MAN OF STEEL

TO THE MEN OF STEEL..
WHO MAKE AMERICA STRONG

A smiling McDonald leaves the White House after delivering the reply of the United Steelworkers of America, CIO, in the 1946 wage dispute.

Man Of Steel

THE STORY OF DAVID J. McDONALD

George Kelly and Edwin Beachler

Edward

NORTH AMERICAN BOOK CO. • NEW YORK

FOREWORD

SHORTLY BEFORE HE DIED, Philip Murray planned with Benjamin Fairless of the United States Steel Corporation to make a series of joint visits to steel plants of the Corporation. The purpose was to show in a concrete way that these top leaders of management and labor believed that they had more to gain by working together than at cross purposes; that the real interests of management and labor were identical and not opposite.

Unhappily, Mr. Murray passed away before he could make any of these visits. But, fortunately, his successor, David J. McDonald, the subject of the biography *Man of Steel,* was able to take up where Philip Murray left off. These visitations began in November, 1953.

Of course they are mainly symbolic. But they vividly express Mr. Murray's concept of the ultimate stage in the development of a collective bargaining relationship: the recognition of the mutuality of interest of management and labor.

Dave McDonald belongs to the same school of collective bargaining, as well he might. He was at Philip Murray's side from the very beginning of the Union as the Steel Workers Organizing Committee in 1936. Like Mr. Murray, he had first-hand knowledge of the earlier stages in the development of the relationship between the United Steel Workers and the steel industry. He was in the front lines during the battle for recognition in 1937. He was at the collective bargaining table as the union hammered out clause by clause the first rudimentary contract. He was on the picket line during the strikes to gain the high level of wages, working conditions, and pensions the steelworkers have now attained.

These were not easy battles. There was bloodshed, as well as sweat and tears. Feelings ran high. To the everlasting credit of the union and the industry, their leaders emerged from these conflicts with no residual hostilities. In the brief space of fifteen years, the great steel industry moved from practically no union representation to practically one hundred percent organization. The complex problems presented as a result are almost incredible to contemplate in retrospect. Yet even more incredible is the manner in which they have been solved.

The constructive development of management-labor relations in the steel industry has importance far beyond this huge, basic, and essential industry. It has been said that as steel goes so goes the nation. That is certainly true in the field of labor relations. The progress of collective bargaining in the steel industry has invariably set the pace for the rest of the country. Consequently, the quality of leadership on both the union and management side of the table has been of infinite value to the entire country. That is why the people of this nation can feel mighty pleased and satisfied that the progressive and forward looking leadership of Philip Murray has been followed by a man who stands for the same sound principles of American trade unionism.

I receive particular satisfaction in viewing the great collective bargaining accomplishments in the steel industry. In a sense it represents the ultimate fulfillment of the basic objectives of the original National Labor Relations Act of 1935. That law is sometimes called the Wagner Act because of its sponsorship by my father, the late Senator Robert F. Wagner. The main goal of that law, too often lost sight of in the course of its stormy history, was to "encourage the practice and procedure of collective bargaining." It was not, as its critics would have you believe, a pro-labor law. It was a pro-collective bargaining law. It was avowedly designed to help get unions *to* the bargaining table. But once *at* the bargaining table, they were on their own.

My father believed fervently in the process of collective bargaining. He knew that it was the only way in a democracy for labor and management to deal with each other. He was convinced that it could be made to work. Yet, at the time the Wagner Act was passed, the vast bulk of American industry was entirely unfamiliar with the practice and procedure of collective bargaining.

If it could be made to work in American industry, then it would, my father believed, act as a bulwark for the protection of our entire American way of life. The steel industry, more than any other, was the testing ground of this important concept. It was to prove whether or not the faith of my father and those associated with him in sponsoring a pro-collective bargaining law was justified.

Today, as we see the heads of the great Steelworkers Union and the Steel Corporation jointly visit the steel plants of that Corporation as two closely associated members of the same team, we know that the Wagner Act has fulfilled its mission.

But collective bargaining is a dynamic process. It never stands still, no more than any component of our great industrial machine. And, like all complex mechanisms, it

takes careful watching. Neither labor nor management can
ever afford to be casual about their mutual relationships.
They must continually work at the job of working together.

The publication of *Man of Steel* is most timely. The
death of the beloved Philip Murray marked the end of an
era. This era saw the union grow from a handful of members to a mighty organization of over one million. It saw
an unorganized industry first grant recognition and then
establish collective bargaining relationships with the Steelworkers Union. But the rich harvest of the ploughing and
the planting involved in winning recognition and bargaining rights has yet to be reaped. With his knowledge and in-
sight into the past, the youthful, energetic Dave McDonald is uniquely equipped to lead this million strong into
the future.

It is only by studying the past that we can justify even
an attempt to predict the future. The story of the future
in steel is to be found in the book *Man of Steel,* a study of
Dave McDonald's part in the great crusade for recognition and collective bargaining in steel. And the history of
the last fifteen years revealed in this book foretells for steel
an era of good will, good relations, good wages, good conditions, and yes, good profits for the steelworkers and the
steel industry under the able leadership of Dave McDonald and his counterparts on the industry side.

Robert F. Wagner
Mayor of the City of New York

January 7, 1954

PREFACE

THE YEAR 1953 was a significant year in steel.

A new world production record for a single year was established when the nation's 1,300 steelmaking furnaces topped all previous marks and headed toward 112 million tons, at year's end.

Even more remarkable were the events of Saturday, November 28th in Pittsburgh—the Steel Capital of the World.

Labor and management sat down to dinner in honor of David J. McDonald, President of the United Steelworkers of America, CIO.

In Pittsburgh's long steelmaking history, none would have been so bold as to predict that some day the titular head of "Big Steel" would join with other industry leaders in tribute to a deserving labor leader.

Now, Benjamin F. Fairless, Chairman of the Board of United States Steel who was touring the company's plants with McDonald, said that labor and management are "inseparably bound together in a state of economic matrimony."

At that dinner, too, was Robert F. Wagner, Jr., then Mayor-elect of New York City, whose illustrious father, the late U.S. Senator, had given labor its Magna Carta in the Wagner Act which became law in 1935.

Surely this was "democratic capitalism" in action. Labor truly had come a long way. New leadership was, perhaps, pointing the way to a brighter future; to industrial peace based on better understanding. There was a promise of far better things than had been known in our industrial democracy at any time past.

This book is about a leading exponent of "democratic capitalism"—David J. McDonald, President of the United Steelworkers of America, CIO.

Perhaps we may be permitted to say, in a lighter vein, that our material was not easily come by.

To say that our subject was uncooperative would be untrue. But to suggest that he was frequently unavailable, in the short time allotted to us, would be a monument of understatement.

Our pursuit of "the McDonald" led one of us to leap a lifting gangplank and follow him to Europe on the S.S. *United States*.

At one point, we facetiously considered changing the working title of the book from "Man of Steel" to "man in motion." But it was, all in all, an interesting and pleasurable task.

We wish to acknowledge with sincere appreciation the help of Mrs. David J. McDonald, Mrs. Joseph Irr, Joseph McDonald, Arthur Grant, Edward M. Durkin, Leslie Weiner, James W. Trullinger, Robert E. McCormick, Frederic A. Wadsworth, and William R. Tighe.

GEORGE KELLY
EDWIN H. BEACHLER

Pittsburgh, Pa.
January, 1954

CONTENTS

INTRODUCTION

THROUGH THE shadowy woodland of Pennsylvania, the night train from Washington, D. C., unfurled a ribbon of light. It surged onward, piercing the black-carpeted valleys and rivers.

Inside the club car, two men talked earnestly as the train clattered around the mountains of the Allegheny chain, approaching the great Pittsburgh mills. Hoarse blasts of the whistle intruded on their conversation. The train slowed to a crawl.

Suddenly, the windows blazed with reflections from the Bessemer converters of the Braddock mills.

The older man, white-haired with dark bushy eyebrows, pointed at the brilliant glow and said:

"There's our objective, David!"

The younger man turned a handsome head topped with wavy brown hair. He peered out the window and nodded. Then he brought his pipe up and puffed, knowing his companion would continue.

"You and I are going to organize those mills, David," the older man declared.

"As you know, John L. Lewis wants me to be head of the steelworkers and—"

He stopped and surveyed the calm young man to relish the full effect of his words.

"You, David, are going to be secretary-treasurer of the new organization."

This time the young man gulped hard before he nodded. His vigorous reaction pleased the older man, but he waved down any reply.

"Yes, David, there lies the stricken giant of labor. We are going to revive those mills and the men in them . . .

We are men of steel . . . I am rough and you are polished steel . . . You had the benefits of a college education . . . We will make a good team . . . Together, we will do this thing that everyone thinks can't be done."

That was June 10, 1936.

The next day, Philip Murray became chairman and David J. McDonald secretary-treasurer of the Steel Workers Organizing Committee.

Within a week, they kicked off the greatest organizing drive in the history of labor. It was a drive that was to shake the entire country and lift unionism to undreamed-of heights.

Seemingly, neither Murray nor McDonald had ever heard of the cynical edict—"You'll never organize steel."

With Murray calling the plays and McDonald putting them into action, the committee of eleven organizers lifted the stricken giant to its feet within five years.

These men who were to make history held their first meeting on June 17, 1936, in Pittsburgh. When the late afternoon shadows began to fall, they had completed the pattern for the campaign and were ready with a formal statement of policy.

It was curiously free of emotion for men who could remember the bloody history of the steel worker in America and were about to throw down the gage of battle:

"The Steel Workers Organizing Committee wishes at the outset of this campaign to explain its main objective and the spirit of responsibility to the whole labor movement and to the nation in which it is undertaking the gigantic task of organizing the steel industry" . . .

So it began.

The CIO United Steelworkers of America, as the union

came to be known, emerged during the post-war years as the most powerful labor force in the world.

By mid-1953, membership had grown to a whopping 1,180,000 and was still climbing.

Because of the dynamic leadership which it presented and the basic nature of the industry it served, the USA became the pacesetter for all unions. It was steel that set the pattern for the seven rounds of nationwide wage increases gained since the close of World War II.

In mid-1953, the American Iron and Steel Institute reported that average hourly earnings of 696,000 iron and steel workers had hit a new all-time high of $2.31. On top of this were social security, insurance, pensions and other "fringe" benefits. This compared with a base wage of 66 cents an hour when the SWOC began its recruiting drive.

During the first seven months of 1953, the payroll was estimated at $1,959,372,000, almost equal to the payroll for the entire year of 1947. And the average work week was forty hours.

Heading this parade of progress for the men in the mills was Dave McDonald, the new "Man of Steel."

The fifty-year-old Pittsburgher stepped into the Presidency of the steelworkers on November 15, 1952, following the death of Philip Murray. Although his services to the cause of labor were relatively unknown and unsung, Dave had labored in the labor vineyard with Murray for thirty years. First, as personal secretary, then as secretary-treasurer of the United Steelworkers.

As first lieutenant of the elder labor statesman, Dave carried the heavy behind-the-scenes load. He organized and ran the conventions, pulled the administrative, collective bargaining and organizing strings, and did all the other numerous things which kept the USA house in order.

In a very real way, his light had been hidden under a

bushel. His job was to keep Murray out front. Even his severest critics acknowledged that he had played a strong role in shaping the course of labor. However, it was not until he succeeded to the Presidency that the wraps were thrown off, revealing a dynamic leader who had been loyally straddling a difficult situation like a Colossus.

No one of his years has played a bigger role!

Born, bred, and schooled in the union movement, he cut his "eye-teeth" in the bitter United Mine Workers' struggles of the 1920's.

McDonald had first-hand knowledge of the methods by which the Communists knifed the miners during the 1925–27 strikes. He was the first CIO official to speak out against the Reds in 1937.

Along with organizing the steelworkers, he has had more experience in the international field than any other American labor figure. Schooled both in the mills and colleges, Dave McDonald is the prototype of the new look in labor leaders.

This "new look" is not a matter of appearance, or the fullness of his educational and mill background. It is a matter of attitude, method and temperament. Unlike the oldstyle labor officials, who became successful by banging away at management at every turn, McDonald takes a smoother approach . . . talking boldly about new ideas and subjects that once were banned in labor circles. It is true that times have changed, and with that change has come a new climate in labor-management relations. Nevertheless, McDonald's versatility, his change of pace to suit any situation, are real assets to those he serves.

His views on strikes, capitalism, international labor, world peace, changes of the machine age, are just as fresh and arresting as they are forthright.

Most of the time, he is thinking one jump ahead of the

rest of the field. That is a canny faculty, admired by his adversaries and appreciated by his staff.

Although trained by years on the firing line and still handy at the rough-and-tumble, he prefers the peaceful course of negotiating at the collective bargaining table. Suave, subtle and smart—choose your adjective and your occasion—he can hold his own in any company.

Dave measures up to that "new look" in appearance, too. He even came close to a Hollywood job with Warner Brothers, some years back, when he was offered an assistant director's berth. No one who knows him can doubt that he would have made a brightly burnished name for himself whether he worked in front or back of the cameras.

Unlike old-style labor leaders who thought it desirable to put up a "poor front," McDonald goes first-class everywhere. He is always dressed for the occasion. He is a fine figure of a man, standing a broad-shouldered 200 pounds with his now silvery hair as wavy as ever to set off his handsome features. He is enough to set the hopeful hearts a-thumping in any feminine group.

One thing that is a heritage of the past—one thing he has in common with all the hard-bitten steelworkers who ever served labor, is his unswerving self-dedication to the cause of men who work for a living. Striving to achieve the best possible in life for all steelworkers, Dave feels their officers should set the pace.

While he acknowledges he is most at home in a union hall, observers will tell you he is equally at ease with civic leaders, statesmen, or in Pittsburgh's exclusive Duquesne Club or New York's Union League Club.

Labor's affairs have become big business, he will tell you, needing the administrative attention of any large business in order to live up to its new position and responsibilities.

Every time he speaks as President of the United Steel-workers, more than 5,000,000 people are direct participants in the statements and may be affected. The union is a multi-million dollar a year operation—a big league business, indeed.

On a trip to Europe aboard the swift new liner, S.S. *United States,* in October, 1953, David J. McDonald summed up the changes which have come to labor, a transition which nothing epitomizes more than his own life:

"Nobody was poorer than I was . . . 'Dave,' my mother would say, 'run down to Mrs. Smith's and get a dime's worth of boiling meat' . . . and even that was a rare meal. . . .

"Now on the S.S. *United States,* I'm a V.I.P. Not too many years ago I was lower in the social and economic scale than the ship's bilge. That's how far labor has come today. People now look up to a labor official for what he represents; for what he has done to improve the lot of millions of people.

"The leaders of industry are beginning to understand why you've got to spread around the emoluments of manufacture. What the hell good is there to make something unless a man can buy it and use it?

"If I have made one little, tiny contribution . . . I hope I have helped make it possible for a working man's family to have a steak on the table . . . even just once in a while.

"But if you were never really hungry, you can't appreciate how important that is."

Then he strides off along the deck at a brisk pace with the wind blowing his jacket. Sparks fly back mingling with pipe smoke that quickly disappears in the Atlantic air. Watching him, you decide that mass of movement adds up to a man on a mission . . . every waking hour.

8

CHAPTER 1

SCOTCH BOTTOMS

THE CRAGGY HILLS and steel stacks of Hazelwood poke up along the Monongahela River just a few miles from Pittsburgh's Point. Normally, the river runs red and yellow, reflecting the awesome creation of the chimneys and furnaces lining its bank like weird fortresses.

Almost every night of the year, the whirls and flashes could pick out sternwheelers pushing barge fleets loaded with coal. But this night, the rivermen must look to the channel lights on the bridges. The inshore waters are dark beside the mills.

It was November 22, 1902. David John McDonald, named for his father, howled his way into the world at a bleak hour. Steelworker McDonald, local union secretary in the old Amalgamated Association of Tin, Iron and Steelworkers which his newborn son was destined to take over and lift to the heights, was out on strike.

9

In the little frame house on Flowers Avenue, David and Mary McDonald greeted the arrival of their first born with mixed emotions. The specter of hunger, hardship, and a fruitless deadlock cast a heavy shadow on the home. But Steelworker McDonald was hardened to labor troubles and confident that the struggle would be won eventually.

Almost all steelworkers shared his confidence, belying the opinion expressed exactly ten years earlier by H. C. Frick following the surrender of the Homestead workers. On November 22, 1892, Frick gleefully cabled Carnegie in Scotland:

> Strike officially called off yesterday (November 21, 1892). Our victory is now complete and most gratifying. Do not think we will ever have any serious labor trouble again . . . we had to teach our employees a lesson and we have taught them one they will never forget.

Perhaps it was a portent that today's President of the United Steelworkers was born on this anniversary. Also, that Phil Murray arrived from Scotland that same year.

It was not due to short memories, however, that Steelworker McDonald and his fellows were on strike. Homestead would rank as the bloodiest day in American labor history for years to come. Its widows and orphans would remember, too. No, these were tough-minded men who dreamed they might outlive their bondage. Even the threat of death at the hands of hired Pinkertons could not cow

10

men whose will had been forged by the 12-hour day and the brutal 24-hour turn once every two weeks.

Steelworker McDonald had no love for the clusters of frame dwellings that climbed the sooty hills from the bottoms close by the mill. This was one of the black towns of Pennsylvania. Slack crunched under your feet on the wooden porch floor. At times, when the mills blew out the stacks, the dusty slack darkened the smoke-laden sky to night hue. Wives swept and scrubbed and washed futilely, but the shiny bits of ore were always there—in your eyes, seeping down your turned-up coat collar. You tasted it, lived with it, and sullenly endured it—always hoping.

A native of Ireland, this striking Senior Dave McDonald had hopped into the iron mills of Wales at the age of 12. Then, feeling that a young man could find greater opportunity in the United States, he had worked his way across the Atlantic at the age of 16.

So far, the fortune-seeking trip had brought nothing but trouble and uncertainty. His first job in the steel mills of Springfield, Ill., where he joined the Knights of Labor, ended abruptly during a strike. Chased out of town and told not to return, he rode the rods to Pittsburgh. His luck turned for the better, briefly, on landing a job in the Hazelwood mill. This later became the Continental mill of the National Tube Company and since has been torn down.

Even if his job were lost again in the latest strike, Steelworker McDonald was determined that his son would have a brighter future. Equally determined was his wife—Mary

11

Kelly McDonald. Her roots extended deep into a clan of Irish labor leaders who battled for the advancement of the working man for more than half a century. Her father was Patrick Kelly, who emigrated from Ireland in time for the Civil War. Settling in Sharon, Penna., he helped build the Sharon Steel Works. Then joined the "Knights of Vulcan" and became secretary of that pioneer labor union.

Her brothers, John and Jim Kelly, also were prominent in the labor movement. John held an office in Local 3, A. F. of L., Bridge, Ornamental and Structural Iron Workers which still is in operation. Jim belonged to the Amalgamated Association.

The arrival of her first son in the midst of a strike might have worried a less courageous woman. But Mary Kelly McDonald, a devout Catholic and outspoken labor crusader all her life, had faith in the future.

Looking back, the President of the United Steelworkers of America, CIO, likes to recall that, instead of a silver spoon:

"I was born with a union spoon in my mouth. Unionism was inbred in me."

Shortly after Dave's birth, the McDonald family moved from Flowers Avenue into a brick row house on Rutherglen Street in Scotch Bottoms. This was an Irish community then, but since has become a mixture of nationalities and races. The area today is the site of a multi-million-dollar expansion of the Jones and Laughlin Steel Corporation's Hazelwood Works.

Young Dave's earliest recollections begin in that center house of the brick row of three. It was heated by a pot-bellied stove and lighted by oil lamps.

In Scotch Bottoms, the family expanded. After Dave came Joseph, four years younger, who is now Assistant Director for the United Steelworkers Political Action Committee. There also were two sisters, Mary, who died in 1932, and Margaret, now Mrs. Joseph Irr, who lives in the Brookline section of Pittsburgh.

Dave made his first appearance as a public performer at the tender age of four years, while living in Scotch Bottoms. His dad had taken him to the neighborhood butcher shop. In a glow of paternal pride, he stood the youngster up on the counter. After considerable prodding, Dave recited "Little Fishies in the Brook." The butcher and several customers applauded vigorously.

The result was hardly what the approving audience expected. Upset by all the attention, the young speaker burst into tears.

Perhaps this reaction was an early indication of an extremely practical mind at work. Dave had already discovered that public speaking was not the most persuasive weapon for a small boy in Scotch Bottoms. As for the elder McDonald, if he felt that Dave could be a success on the platform he was gifted with foresight.

Even before he learned his three R's, young Dave received lessons in the ABC's of the union movement. Troubles of the men who worked in the mills were never ending. They made the daily conversation of his mother and father. Grandmother Catherine Kelly and his uncles frequently chipped in their experiences and views. Often enough, the men of the family were coming home with bumps and bruises, the result of backing their enthusiasm for union issues with their fists.

Wives knew just how unpopular the unions were in those days. Spies and spotters interfered with even the social mingling of neighbors. When a man called, he might be a friend come to visit, or a foe come seeking information on organizing activity. Dave's mother would report at the family fireside, on more than one occasion:

"Some of the women are afraid to be seen talking with me, poor dears. They're afraid that the company won't like it, what with me being the wife of a union organizer."

All this was during the period of the decline of the Amalgamated Association, following the ill-fated Homestead Steel riots of 1892. "Scabs" and "Pinkerton killers" became household words of scorn.

Oddly enough, it was Dave's mother—not the men of the family—who dominated the discussions about the plight of workers in the mills. When "Aunt Mary," or "Aunt Mame," as she was variously known, swept into a crowd, she immediately took the spotlight. A striking Irish beauty, with wavy, light brown hair, she led the front room struggle "to improve the lot of the steelworkers."

14

Any woman who watched the shifts go and come would need a cast-iron heart not to cry out with pity on occasion as the hollow-eyed hulks returned from the hell of noise, heat and gruelling labor. These were men who walked with their heads down. They went home to food and bed.

So it went on, seven days a week. Day turn, night turn; night turn, day turn. Hope was a hard thing to hold fast. The goal was survival.

Instead of the "Three Bears and Goldilocks," Mother McDonald told her children exciting and suspenseful stories of how her father had to sneak off to the woods for union meetings. They were exciting stories, meant to impress the children with the need to improve their lot with education. Also, to teach them the hard facts of life which govern the lot of a steelworker's family. It was difficult for the children to understand "why grandpa couldn't hold meetings at home." As they grew older, they understood more easily why union meetings would not be permitted in the public halls of Sharon or any other place. Children learn fast.

It seemed exciting to know, too, that Grandpa Kelly had to hide his books on labor unions in the basement for fear of the consequences of their being seen.

"It's just like the smugglers' cave, isn't it, Mother?" little Joe once suggested.

Still later, when they had begun school, the boys perplexed their mother with a question. It was a real stumper. Dave brought it up.

15

"Mother," he said, "in school, we're told to read as much as we can. Why can't people read about unions?"

Right up until her death at the age of 75 years in 1945, Mary Kelly McDonald never lost her zest for the "union movement." She was an ardent champion of Franklin Delano Roosevelt.

The struggle of raising a family through strikes and strife cost her dearly. But she never complained or wavered.

During the 1907 depression—or panic—the McDonald family moved to St. Clair Borough. This was near Mt. Oliver in Pittsburgh's South Hills, across the always murky Monongahela.

By that time, most of the old steel unions had been broken. Dave's father decided to follow John F. Kelly, Manus Gallagher, and other friends who left the mill to go into the saloon business. But, where his friends made money, the elder McDonald discovered too late that he picked the wrong spot.

His saloon, opened with the aid of a few borrowed dollars from friends, was located in the center of St. Clair's almost solidly German community. The McDonalds were the only Irish family and couldn't "Sprechen Sie Deutsch."

In those days, nationality lines formed barriers more impregnable than steel. Pittsburgh's great "melting pot" simply wasn't ready to melt just yet.

So, the McDonalds found themselves jumping from hot

mill conditions into the struggle of how to operate a saloon without any customers.

Soon after moving into the house at the corner of Mountain and Ormsby Streets, the family was hit with another trouble—very serious illness. Curly-headed Dave, at the age of five, came down with spinal meningitis. He recovered after weeks in bed, but it left him skinny and weak for several years.

Playing a vital role in his recovery was a violin. The youngster observed Nicky, a barber, fiddling in his shop across the street. This intrigued him.

"Oh boy, if I could just have one of those," he told his parents with eyes shining. They, somehow, scraped up enough money to buy a violin. And Nicky, in his spare time between haircuts, obliged by giving free lessons.

Dave's first solo number was "I Want a Girl Just Like the Girl That Married Dear Old Dad." It became the neighborhood theme song, a number for any and every occasion.

This launched him on an interest in music that ranged from jive up to long-hair symphonies and operas in later life.

In the midst of his violin craze, Dave passed his sixth birthday and in 1909 headed for school. His first day produced the most bewildering experience of his life. Reporting to St. Joseph's Parochial School, he couldn't understand a thing that was being said. At lunch, the completely baffled youngster trooped home and told his mother:

17

"I don't know what they're saying. I'm not going back."

His mother had different ideas. She marched him back in the afternoon to see the pastor. Discovering that all the classes were conducted in German, she decided to send Dave to the Spring Lane Public School.

Dave put up a "holy howl." He wasn't going to any public school. He figured that, being a Catholic, if he didn't go to a parochial school, he wouldn't have to go at all. The idea appealed to him.

There was another march. This time to the public school. Dave sweated it out until lunchtime. On the way home, he stopped at a culvert near the bridge. He decided he wouldn't go home or back to school either. He played hooky that afternoon. With night coming on, the wind cut through his thin jacket. Cold and hungry, he sheepishly slipped into the house through the cellar, but his mother was waiting at the top of the steps with a large paddle.

This took the chill out of him, but did not alter his views about school one bit.

Two paddlings a day followed for a week—one in the morning to send him on his way, the other after lunch to encourage him to return for the afternoon session.

Dave finally was convinced that his plan to avoid school wasn't so good after all. He surrendered.

However, not until second grade did the reluctant student become more than that. The turning point came with trouble over "double EES" and "double FFS."

18

Dave trekked home one day and attempted to tell his mother about the trouble he was having. She was completely mystified until a neighbor boy explained:

"Oh, Dave is supposed to write 'coffee' ten times. He missed it in spelling class today—spelled it with only one 'f' and one 'e.' "

After some strenuous sessions with his mother, the reluctant student finally learned how to spell the word with double letters.

This accomplishment made him so proud that it changed his whole attitude about school. It gave him confidence to dig into his lessons. And within a few years, he forged to the top of the class.

At the same time, Dave also developed into a pretty handy lad with his fists. Gradually, he was shaking off the effects of spinal meningitis.

Many a brawl occurred in his backyard over cherries and apples from the fruit trees.

One youngster, who had been clobbered by young McDonald, came wailing to the door with his mother.

"Just look what your ruffian did to my son," the woman screamed, "his nose is bloody."

Mother McDonald, busy patching a cut on Dave's head, calmly pointed to the wound and snorted:

"Shurr, and I suppose my boy did this to himself. Now be off with you and let the lads have their fun."

That one was a stand-off. But Dave, sprouting up like

19

a June cornstalk, dished out considerably more than he absorbed.

After he finished third grade at Spring Lane, the Mc-Donalds moved back to Hazelwood into a house on Chatswood Avenue. The saloon business folded that summer and his father returned to steelworking in the Jones and Laughlin mill on the South Side.

Everyone was happier, especially his mother, to get back with old Irish friends. They lived in a double frame house, next to the McGirrs.

Dave soon learned that the McGirr girl played the piano. He was still taking violin lessons. So, they occasionally hooked up in a musical duet through the walls of the duplex. More often, though, it was a battle of music.

On one occasion, the McGirr girl recruited Dave, along with other neighboring youngsters, to sing in a recital. He didn't last until the performance. She booted him out for disrupting the rehearsals.

"I didn't want to be in her old show anyhow," he confided to his mother. "That's a bunch of sissy stuff."

Some years later Dave changed his mind about that— to the extreme of studying in Carnegie Tech's drama school and seriously considering a Hollywood career.

Even then, at the age of nine, his musical talent was asserting itself. He sang in the "Surplus Choir" as the boys called it, because they wore surplices, at St. Stephen's Church. Through two-hour-long processions of "Forty Hours" devotions and during Holy Week, Dave chanted old Latin hymns and developed a serious interest in his Catholic religion.

Sometimes, though, the priest had to admonish the boys to say the Latin chant "Libera nos Domine" a little more distinctly. It sounded suspiciously, at times, like "Leave Her on a Stormy Day."

Dave took considerable pride in "leading out the third pew." This was no small honor, handling the assignment of starting the boys down from the altar at just the right time at the end of Mass.

In the fourth grade at St. Stephen's Parochial School in Hazelwood, young McDonald developed into a top-notch student. He ranked 1-2-3-4 with Maurice Porter and two girls, Madeline Delehanty and Regina Reynolds. They took turns leading the class.

If he didn't make a grade of 98 (out of a possible 100) in any subject, it irked him, and he would plug away until reaching that mark. Rarely, though, did studies interfere with his ball playing.

Every afternoon, Dave would race home after school and get the games organized. His talent for organizing took root in those games. His first good friend, Howard Hague, a boy who lived a block away, helped round up the gang. Howard still is with him as an assistant in the United Steelworkers of America.

Many a rousing football game was staged on the unpaved street in front of the McDonald home. Dave played

21

in the line, blocking and tackling much as he was to do later in the labor movement for Philip Murray.

Stalwarts in those knock-down grid battles included his younger brother, Joe, who later starred as halfback for St. Roselia High School in Greenfield and as fullback for Elmer Layden's Duquesne University teams in the late 1920's; Bud Flanagan and Cliff Ryan, who became all-scholastic linemen.

During the baseball sessions, the McDonald gang moved up to a steep field on the hillside. It took quite an uphill wallop to put one out of the lot. Dave, a strong hitter, got more than his share.

In fifth grade, his sports and school activities, as well, were curtailed by an attack of appendicitis. Dave shook that off and it was the last major illness until, in his late forties, his left ear suddenly went deaf while a guest at the horse races at Wheeling Downs in West Virginia. The ear ailment was attributed to extensive flying and doctors ordered him grounded. Always ready with a quip, Dave told the medical men he could account for the sudden impairment:

"That's the ear in which the touts whispered their bum tips."

FIRST LABOR TROUBLES

Troubles piled up for the McDonald family with the arrival of World War I.

Dave's father was stricken with pneumonia in the epidemic that brought death and suffering to thousands in the Pittsburgh area.

During the long months that the elder McDonald was out of work and fighting for his life, the family had a "divvil" of a time scraping up enough money on which to live.

They existed largely on corn-meal mush and pancakes—the only fare they could afford during strikes and other troubles such as this. With four growing youngsters to feed, sometimes there wasn't enough of that to go around. Dave's mother darned and redarned old socks, put patches on top of patches to keep knees and elbows from poking through.

23

Then, an even greater blow struck the family. Shortly after recovering from pneumonia, Dave's father suffered a severe injury while working in the No. 9 rolling mill at the South Side plant. A piece of steel, coming through a roll, sheared off and ripped through his leg.

It required a six-month siege in South Side Hospital to repair his shattered limb.

The injury provided young Dave with a grim introduction to the subject of Workmen's Compensation. That was before Pennsylvania adopted the Workmen's Compensation Law.

Burned deeply into his mind was the need to help people in a plight such as this. During visits to the hospital with his mother, they talked constantly about the need for assistance.

And at home they lived with the hardship every day. The family was "absolutely broke." Not a penny in the house. Bills piled up. Credit was shut off. Dave longed for "ten cents' worth of boiling meat" which the family usually could afford on Sunday.

Somehow, his mother managed to keep things going. She took in washing. The boys picked up a few pennies at odd jobs.

"At times," Dave recalls, "the family had incredible bits of luck."

Once, when there was nothing to eat, Joe came tearing home just as fast as his legs would carry him. He had found a dollar bill in a puddle of water.

"We really were in business that day."

Along with the struggle to survive, Dave was having his own troubles in school. From fifth grade, he had jumped into the seventh, along with Maurice, Madeline, and Regina—the other three top students in the class.

This required a good deal of extra study to fill in the gaps of the sixth grade studies he had skipped.

Even with his father in the hospital, the family didn't miss Christmas that desperate year. They never did.

His mother scraped up enough to buy two 10-cent periscopes at the five and ten cent store for the boys.

It was a Christmas Dave never forgot.

He and Joe, peering out from behind trees through their periscopes, refought Civil War battles on the hill near their home.

The hill was known as "Fort Black" during the Civil War, and "Fort White" lay on the other side of the Monongahela. Built by Union forces to ward off Confederate raids, the forts never served their expected purpose.

But the McDonald troops in Hazelwood put "Fort Black" to good use that winter. Dave and Joe dug caves into the steep mountainside, climbed trees and kept firing away. Many an imaginary Confederate bit the dust.

They were Union soldiers all the way. The outcome never was in doubt.

One bleak afternoon, while digging into the hillside, Dave found an old revolver that likely belonged to some

25

Union officer. At least, that's the story he told the other boys in his outfit.

He then was a real big wheel, leading the charges up the slopes brandishing a real revolver instead of a 10-cent cap pistol.

It little mattered that the barrel was choked with rust and the handle wouldn't turn. Huh! Nobody else had a real Civil War pistol.

An even bigger thrill awaited him in eighth grade the following year of 1916. Dave, at the age of 13, finished in a tie with Madeline Delehanty for top class honors.

However, there were no graduation ceremonies in those days. Everyone at St. Stephen's just said "so long" and went on to high school or jobs.

That fall, Dave entered Holy Cross High School in the South Side. By this time, he was a rangy 145-pounder with legs that almost never stopped running.

It was a long haul to school, several miles from Hazelwood across the river to the South Side.

His father got him a pass to use the Jones and Laughlin hot metal bridge. That saved considerable time, as he ran down Second Avenue, over the bridge, and on out Carson Street to the school.

He could have taken a trolley, but there was no money for carfare.

Dave was just about the only outsider at Holy Cross. He wanted to go there to continue his schooling under the

26

Sisters of Charity—the same Catholic order of teachers who conducted classes at St. Stephen's.

However, he made friends easily. On his long romps through the South Side, he got to know just about everyone in this teeming mill section.

They immediately liked this good-looking Irish kid with the unruly hair, ready wit and broad grin.

In school, he plugged away at typing, shorthand, bookkeeping, Latin and algebra. Near the end of a two-year commercial course, an opening at Jones and Laughlin's South Side plant was offered to him.

Jobs were hard to get and the family was having tough sledding. So, 15-year-old McDonald, four months before the scheduled June graduation, swapped his books for a job in the polishing mill office.

His first steady job paid an eye-bulging 22 cents an hour. He worked 11 hours a day, six days a week, for a $14.52 paycheck. The hours ran from 7 A.M. to 6:20 P.M., with only 20 minutes off for lunch. He pounded on a typewriter, wrote up orders, and ran errands to all parts of the plant, at top speed all the time.

Never satisfied to stand still, Dave began looking around for a better job. The overwhelming ambition that later spurred him to work off his high school credits and advance through college by night school, brought results within a few months.

He landed a job in the storeroom of National Tube Company's Continental Works. This plant was the suc-

27

cessor to the Hazelwood mill in which his father had worked on arriving in Pittsburgh. The plant had an iron rolling mill, pipe mills, and socket shop for connecting pipe.

Dave, too young for military service at 15, replaced a fellow who had entered service. The new storekeeping job paid 36 cents an hour, a boost of 14 cents. The hours were the same, 66 a week.

It was hard work running up and down the stairs in the three-story and basement plant, lugging items of every description—doing anything that no one else wanted to do. But Dave was "full of beans." He ran until his legs ached and cramped at night so badly that he couldn't sleep.

Each day, though, his boss, John Burns, would wind them up again with words of encouragement.

When the regular storekeeper returned from service at the end of World War I, Dave transferred to the machine shop tool room with the rating of machinist helper. He learned to operate small mechanical saws, drill presses, a small lathe and other equipment.

Eager to keep climbing, he helped machinists set up their jobs, then went on to tackle mechanics. Soon, he could figure gear ratios for cutting threads. Machinists eventually came to him for help. He was a smart boy and knew the answers.

An engineer taught him how to make blueprints. From

28

these, Dave sketched the drawings for jobs the machinists had to turn out.

He also became the unofficial "eye doctor" for the mill. An older hand, Johnny Gallagher, showed him how to remove dirt and shavings from an eye.

The young "Doc" secured a knife with a magnetized blade. Since there was no hospital in the mill, he soon established quite a large practice, and made many friends in the process.

His medical work also got him into trouble with plant officials.

One day, a fellow in the shop suffered a severe eye injury working with a riveting air gun. The hose burst, blowing splinters into his eyes.

Led moaning to the First Aid station, the stricken riveter found no relief. A 65-year-old attendant at the First Aid station, who had been a former plant watchman, didn't know how to remove the blinding splinters. So, he put drops in the pain-racked eyes and sent him back to the shop.

Fellow workers brought the victim, in misery, to see "Doc" McDonald. Dave quickly wheeled him under a bright light and, with a clean handkerchief, removed 18 pieces of wood from one eye.

At this point in the operation, several plant officials pushed their way through the crowd to see what was going on.

One of the officials asked:

"What are you doing, Dave?"

"I'm cleaning out his eye."

"Don't you know you're not allowed to do that?"

"Yes."

"Well, then, cut it out."

"What am I supposed to do—let him go blind?"

"You aren't permitted to do this."

"It's a damn shame there isn't a hospital and nurse to take care of an injured man in this plant. It's a rotten crime."

After this rapid-fire exchange, Dave stormed back to his regular job. But, he returned later and removed 22 more pieces of wood from the injured worker's other eye— for a total of 40 pieces.

All his hell-raising eventually paid off. Within a few months, the plant hired a young doctor and nurse.

However, it did not enhance his popularity with the bosses. They looked upon him as a smart-alec and a pop-off.

Dave was content, though. This was his first real accomplishment. It fired him with ambition to fight for improved working conditions wherever they were needed.

From that time on, Dave had few peaceful moments at work. He constantly was on the warpath and thought more and more about getting out before he was tossed out. But he stayed for five years.

During the 1919 steel strike, when his father walked out of the South Side mill, Dave staged his first sympathy strike. While the National Tube plant wasn't struck or even handbilled, he simply stayed home—giving the excuse that he was ill.

It was his first personal contact with a strike. Although only 17, he attended a rally at Barker's Hall in Hazelwood. The hall was jammed and he stood in the crowd outside listening to "some guy talk at the top of his lungs."

At that time, the steelworkers had no union, no organization. Just a few mechanical trades were organized.

Several months later, back in the National Tube works, Dave had his first brush with socialism—the bandwagon on which the leftwingers were riding in those days.

A blacksmith tried to sell him socialism as the answer to all of the workingman's problems. Dave refused to buy it and they "argued like hell." His parents had conditioned him against it. Rightly or not, they considered socialism to be a great Anti-Catholic movement.

During this period, Conn Duncan, an old master mechanic at National Tube, had the greatest influence on young McDonald. He kept giving him pep talks about going to school.

At home, Dave heard the same thing from his mother and father. They all could point to bitter personal experience and how much better off they would have been with more education.

Gradually, Dave caught the fever for more schooling. His athletic prowess eventually opened the door to a prep school scholarship.

Although never quite a star athlete, he had been developing physically with all his mill work, running instead of riding to the plant and playing ball with independent teams. His lanky 5 foot 10 inch frame filled out to a rugged 175 pounds after he began bringing money home so that the family could eat more substantial food.

Dave had carved out quite a reputation as a hitter. Playing in Pittsburgh's first softball league, organized by the Rev. James Lavelle, a Catholic priest, Dave boomed out 17 homes runs and a robust batting average of .464 in his top season. Although just a fair fielder, he played almost every position—usually catcher, first, or second base. He played ball with "Greenfield Jimmy" Smith, who made the big leagues with the Philadelphia Athletics, and other stars.

In the City League, Dave caught for Greenfield and came within an eyelash of winning the city championship one year.

It was a perfect set-up for hero-making:

Lawrenceville led 2-1 in the last of the ninth.

Two Greenfield men were on base. With two outs, Francie Hammer had singled. Then brother Joe McDonald drew a walk. They represented the tying and winning runs.

It was strictly up to Dave now.

The Lawrenceville pitcher, a stocky fellow with a blinding fast ball, worked carefully to snuff out this last threat.

The count went to two strikes and three balls. Then he poured in the fat one.

Dave belted it sharply over second base.

Hammer and brother Joe, both with speed to burn, lit out for home.

"This wraps it up," Dave thought, as he rounded first and dug in for second base.

Out of the corner of his eye, he saw the centerfielder make the long throw home.

Pulling up at second, Dave turned and saw his brother Joe fly into the plate. Both Joe and the catcher were flat on the ground. The ball was rolling out towards third base.

"We did it," Dave yelled, figuring that the winning run had just crossed the plate.

But he learned later that the umpire ruled Hammer had been tagged out ahead of Joe.

The championship was lost. The game ended in riot. Instead of being a hero, Dave had to be content with a near-miss.

Despite this disappointment, word of his feats on the diamond and sandlot football fields reached Kiski Prep School—famed "incubator" of All-Americans at Saltsburg, Pennsylvania.

Through the efforts of a friend of his father's, Dave was offered a scholarship and chance to play end on Kiski's great football teams of 1920–21.

For a youngster who couldn't muster enough money

for carfare to high school, the opportunity to attend the exclusive prep school seemed too good to be true.

Under Jim Marks—the "Sage of Saltsburg," who, over a quarter century became nationally known as the "only college coach who never coached a college team"—Dave might have gone on to college and gridiron fame on a free ride.

It was the toughest decision of his young life. But he eventually turned down the scholarship because the family needed the income he was earning at the mill. His younger brother, Joe, and sister, Peg, were in high school. And the post-war depression was threatening.

Instead of Kiski, Dave took the long, hard road of mill work and night school. After a year of accounting and other studies at Duquesne University, he shifted to Carnegie Tech's School of Industries. Along with college work, he cleared the balance of his high school studies.

Only a young man of his stamina and determination could have taken the grind.

Rising at 6 o'clock every morning, he worked an 11-hour turn in the Hazelwood mill. After work, he would dash down Second Avenue up through the Greenfield section to his home.

He had to hustle to clean up and change clothes, to make the 7:30 evening class. It always took a fast sprint through Schenley Park to get there on time.

Class lasted until 10:30, then a more leisurely journey

34

home through the park, followed by nightwork to prepare for the next classroom session.

Three nights a week he made this trip. Sometimes, on the way home from work, he was lucky enough to pick up a street car transfer. This saved precious time. With the burden of paying tuition, he couldn't afford street-car-fare.

Often it was past midnight when he fell exhausted into bed for a few short hours before starting the routine all over again the next day.

CHAPTER 3

THE UNION BUG

IN THE BACKWASH of World War I, the "union bug" showed signs of making a comeback. The tide of anti-unionism, although still strong, was receding.

Down in the Hazelwood plant of National Tube Company, Dave McDonald jumped into many a hot argument. In his late 'teens he liked nothing better than a good debate.

With a knack for persuasion, the college student-steelworker took a much more prominent part in the discussions than normally would be permitted any one of his years.

Many of the older men scoffed. Told him he wasn't dry behind the ears. Others, though, liked and respected this earnest kid. He had a new slant on almost any subject.

One of the hotter arguments hinged on whether the miners should take a pay cut.

"The miners ought to take a cut—we took one," was the stock attitude of veteran steelworkers.

"Nuts," Dave argued. "No one should receive less money. The working man isn't making enough now to live on. He's entitled to a bigger share of the products he turns out."

It was during these bitter mill discussions that Dave first heard of John L. Lewis, United Mine Workers' boss whom he was to serve as secretary later and from whom he was to learn many a trick.

Along with the incident of removing splinters from an injured worker's eye, Dave pushed into the thick of other battles in the plant. It earned him the reputation of being one of the leading "workingman voices."

In 1921, the Continental Works was split over the question of the eight-hour day. National Tube officials offered to put it up to a vote. Older workers, however, felt that if the proposal were accepted, it would mean the end of time-and-a-half pay for overtime. They had been receiving about three hours' overtime a week.

Machinist helper McDonald took an opposing view and electioneered for the eight-hour day. He and others sharing the same opinion argued that the company would have to pay a living wage no matter what happened.

This position neither won him any friends nor influenced many people. It put him over the barrel both with management and the old-timers.

The eight-hour day was overwhelmingly defeated. As a minority man, Dave helped count the votes.

"We still lost the overtime rate," he recalls unhappily. "The older men didn't know that was to be in the bargain."

Like Philip Murray, the man he later succeeded as president of the CIO United Steelworkers, it was an argument with a foreman that had most to do with shaping the McDonald career.

In the spring of 1922, flood waters of the Monongahela swept into a section of the Hazelwood mill, a frequent occurrence in those days prior to the building of flood-control dams in the upper river valleys.

Dave was busy grinding drills and making minor repairs on tools. The foreman came into the tool room and told him:

"There's a flood down in the rolling mill. Come on down and help clean it out."

"No, I'm not going to do it," Dave replied. "It's not my job."

The foreman insisted.

The machinist helper again refused.

Still enraged, the foreman told Dave the next day:

"I don't know whether you ought to stay here or not."

That sounded like a pretty good cue to him. He started looking for another job the following morning.

After talking to a railroad employment agent, young McDonald was asked if he could report the following

Monday. Then, the agent, in passing, inquired about his schooling.

Learning that Dave had attended Holy Cross High School, the agent wanted to know:

"Is that Catholic?"

Dave replied that it was.

He never got the job.

It was his first experience with the type of employment practices that have led to the Fair Employment Practices Act.

Next stop was Wheeling Steel Products Company, a subsidiary which since has been absorbed by the Wheeling Steel Corporation.

Sent there by an employment agency, Dave clicked on this one. The job paid $20.00 a week. The hours were better—9 A.M. to 5 P.M., with an hour off for lunch. And Dave was happy.

AWOL, he returned to the Hazelwood mill to gather up his tools, and bumped into his old boss.

"I'm going to fire you," Harry Stroble, superintendent of the machine shop, told him.

"Too late—I quit," the kid machinist helper fired back.

Dave said his goodbyes to the other machinists, gathered up his little box of drawing instruments and tools, and strutted home feeling right proud of himself. He figured five years was long enough to spend in any place without advancing.

The following Monday, he reported for work in the

Wheeling Steel office on the 17th floor of the Oliver Building in Downtown Pittsburgh.

He didn't know it then, but his mill days were gone forever. He became a white collar worker.

In his new job, Dave typed, operated a tumbler switchboard, and served as all-around handyman. Not having touched a keyboard since that brief whirl five years earlier at Jones and Laughlin, he had to brush up on his typing.

Tom Oberhauser, sales manager with a staff of two salesmen, gave him plenty of time to get back into the swing of office life.

The new hand not only managed to get by, but rated his first real vacation that summer of 1922.

His mother maneuvered the household expenses so that she could turn over an entire month's pay of $80.00 to him for a trip to Atlantic City. With Dave nearing his 20th birthday, she thought he deserved a real good time.

With two pals, he had quite a thrill buying the excursion tickets on the Baltimore and Ohio. The trip included stops in Philadelphia and New York.

In Atlantic City, they bunked in a side-street hotel for $18.00 a week including "the eats." The beach and boardwalk opened up a new world to him.

After a week, Dave and one of his pals, Jimmy King, decided to use their ticket privileges and shove on to New York. They were the greenest of rookies in the big town.

As they swaggered out of Pennsylvania Station, with

their straw hats tilted at a sharp angle, a negro porter asked:

"What hotel?"

Dave rattled off the name of a big hotel he had seen on the billboards coming into the city. The porter took a closer look at the new arrivals, shook his head, and said:

"You boys don't want to go there."

He took them to a small hotel on 33rd Street more in keeping with their pocketbook, showed them how to get to Broadway and offered other advice.

Grateful, Dave decided to go all out. He gave the porter a 25-cent tip.

Jimmy and Dave, in a daze, walked miles taking in the sights of New York. They craned their necks at the skyscrapers, spun dizzily in the Times Square rush bewildered by the glittering lights and symphony of noise.

That night their eyes were popping. They shelled out $1.10 for their first Broadway show, "Ziegfeld Follies," starring Will Rogers and Eddie Cantor, in the New Amsterdam Theater.

Cantor's eyes popped back at them.

Dave wanted more of places like New York. He was especially impressed with the Pennsylvania Hotel. It was big, new and wonderful. What's more he felt that, coming from Pennsylvania, this was the hotel for him.

Standing outside and longing to go in, the boys couldn't muster enough nerve. Their finances were running low.

As they turned to go, Dave boasted to Jimmy:

41

"The next time I'm going to stay here."

Like many another confident statement of "the Mc-Donald", that idle boast did come true within the space of two short weeks.

As a final fling, the boys dug up enough money for two bleacher seats at the Polo Grounds to see Muggsy Mc-Graw's fabulous New York Giants.

Then, they piled into a single berth on the sleeper to Pittsburgh. It was a tight fit, but they were riding high all the way home.

CHAPTER 4

TEAMING UP WITH
PHIL MURRAY

ALMOST ANY EVENING in the Summer of 1923,
Dave McDonald could be found with the young Greenfield crowd hanging around McMillin's Drug Store on the
corner of Lydia and Greenfield Avenues. It was their
regular meeting place. In these open-air clubrooms they
engaged in the great American pastime known the world
over as a "bull session."

Opinion was made here—and quoted by the small fry
who worshipped from afar.

Boys of many ages and sizes squatted happily on the
curb, held up telephone poles and an outmoded hitching
post, or stood cross-legged with no other visible means of
support than a stray arm.

There was little formality in Greenfield, and none at all
in this gathering. Usually, they replayed the day's ball

43

game—adding touches which had not occurred to the managers or players. They argued politics, if nothing better turned up to try their powers. And, of course, they interrupted all discourse, from time to time, to whistle at a passing girl.

This was the era of the "Drug Store Cowboy." Restless, searching, and launched to syncopated music. If "collegiate" was youth's theme song, the words were accurate. Trousers then were, indeed, "baggy" and other clothes had a careless look that bordered on "raggy"; life was frothy as whipped cream on a banana split.

The year had its somber notes, too. President Warren G. Harding died in 1923 amid tragic circumstances. Dark clouds were gathering over Washington, hinting of explosive scandals still to come.

Unknown to the eager young man who always commanded attention on the corner, events remote from Greenfield were shaping his destiny.

A gentleman named Elbert H. Gary had made a statement on the 25th of May. Apparently, it had escaped the public events forum which met so regularly at the corner of Lydia and Greenfield Avenues. If so, there were other places where it was discussed at great length and with much heat. These included the mills and union halls of the land. Gary's word was big, discouraging news in Pittsburgh.

Just a little more than two months before the death of President Harding, Gary, famous head of the United States Steel Corporation, had presented the report of a

44

special committee studying working hours in the steel industry. It stifled the thin hopes of America's steel workers.

"Abolition of the 12-hour day in the steel industry," Mr. Gary had reported, "is not now feasible, as it would add 15 per cent to the cost of making steel and would require 60,000 additional workers."

One evening early in September, fate began to tie the skeins together in earnest. Dave joined the gang at the usual place on McMillin's corner. After a tough game at the Greenfield school grounds, he was still breathing hard. Beads of sweat trickled down the side of his face. With an annoyed swipe, he brushed them away.

Never idle for long, the energetic Mr. McDonald began flipping a coin into the lengthening shadows of the corner's telephone pole. The street was now bathed in a reddish glow. He finally missed a catch in the crazy-quilt pattern of sunset and shadows. The coin bounded along the sidewalk and leaped the curb.

Stooping to retrieve it, Dave looked up to find a boyhood pal, Mark Stanton, approaching.

They exchanged laconic "Hi's!" Then Mark said:

"Gee, Dave, I could have gotten a good job today if I wasn't going to study for the priesthood at St. Vincent's this fall."

"Yeh, where?"

"Some fellow by the name of Phil Murray wanted me to be his private secretary."

45

"And who is this Murray?", McDonald wanted to know.

"Why, you ought to know him. He's the vice-president of the Miners' Union."

"Nope never heard of him. But how much did he offer to pay you, Mark?"

"Oh, about two hundred and twenty-five dollars a month."

Dave whistled sharply. That was nearly three times more than he was making at Wheeling Steel. This Murray must be important. He had heard about the miners, of course. Who in Pittsburgh could be unaware of this powerful union that was going places with John L. Lewis in the driver's seat?

As these thoughts flashed through his mind, Dave's manner became earnest.

"Gee whiz, Mark," he confided, "I'd like to take a crack at that job. Who knows Murray?"

Mark Stanton, who ironically, was forced to leave the seminary later after a football injury and now is office secretary of the big Steelworkers' local in the Hazelwood plant of Jones and Laughlin, told him:

"Red Welsh is the man to see."

This was it. The big break Dave had been waiting for. It proved to be the turning point that shaped his life.

All that night, Dave tried to figure a way to approach Welsh, a referee with the Workmen's Compensation Board and a "big shot" in Greenfield. McDonald, not yet 21 and unknown to Welsh, was afraid to barge in without an introduction.

So, he set up headquarters at McMillin's Drug Store, enlisting the help of his friends to find someone who knew Welsh. Dave finally learned that Lawrence (Babe) Keenan might be "the guy who could do it."

Dave knew Babe Keenan pretty well. They had played ball together. Babe, who later became superintendent of the Allegheny County Workhouse, was a local hero. He starred at quarterback for the Bradley Eagles, a big semi-pro team in McKees Rocks. In Greenfield this was more important than starring in the Ivy League.

Tackling the husky quarterback was easy. After a huddle, Babe promised:

"Sure, I know Red, I'll take you in to see him."

The next day, with the town hero clearing the way, Dave finally met Red Welsh. He made a good impression. Red took him down town to the Columbia Bank Building to see UMW official, Dane Hickey.

Hickey said Murray would be in Friday of that week and told McDonald to come back at that time.

Dave rushed home and hauled out his old shorthand books. He "studied like hell," with his sister, Peg, dictating articles. They worked every spare moment the next few days to revive his shorthand.

On Friday, he met Phil Murray.

After Dave told about his family background, education and experience, Murray asked:

47

"Anything else that you have done?"

"Yes, I am president of the Holy Cross High School Alumni Association. Also, I have been going out in the evenings to help organize the Catholic Alumni Association of Pittsburgh."

That did it. Murray was a devout Catholic and he had a high regard for such initiative as McDonald indicated.

"Can you start work Monday?" Dave was asked.

Gulping hard, he murmured:

"Oh, I'd like to at least work out notice for my boss at Wheeling Steel."

"This is the psychological moment," the older man warned. "How about Wednesday? That would give them a two-day notice."

"Fine," the new secretary agreed.

Then, the UMW official told Dave he wanted him to be ready to go to New York that very next week.

Walking out of the Columbia Bank Building, McDonald was floating on clouds. He couldn't feel the steps or be sure there was pavement under his feet. Here he was with a job that paid nearly three times what he was making— much more than he ever hoped to make at the age of 20.

And it was a job in the labor movement. Dave thought how happy his mother and father would be. He recalled how his father once "raised hell" because he had a date with the daughter of a man who had been a scab 20 years before. Now, his parents would be really proud of him.

Somehow, Dave climbed down from the clouds long

enough to get some solid help in shorthand from a neighbor, Grace McCluskey, who lived two doors away.

On Monday, he told his immediate superior, a salesman at Wheeling Steel, that he was leaving.

"You can't do this," the salesman replied.

"Look, I'm going to get $225 a month, compared with $80 here!"

"Well, you sure are leaving us in an awful hole."

Dave suggested the name of a man who could take his place—his boyhood pal, Howard Hague, who was then working in Jones and Laughlin's by-product coke plant in Hazelwood.

With this shift ironed out, everyone was happy. When Dave left, Sales Manager Tom Oberhouser shook hands and said:

"We're sorry to see you go, but congratulate you on this break. You're making a very wise choice."

The next morning, the UMW's new secretary, "just scared to death," walked into the office at 408 Columbia Bank Building to report for work.

He hardly had time to catch his breath.

That same night, Vice-President Murray and Dave, reinforced by a $100 loan from his new boss and $20 from his father, hopped a train for New York.

It was the beginning of an association that spanned almost 30 years and made labor history.

Arriving in New York, Dave found his idle boast of just two weeks earlier coming true. The porter led them through the underground passage into Hotel Pennsylvania—the same fine hotel he had surveyed so longingly.

An even greater thrill came later that same day of September 13, 1923. Vice-President Murray took him down into the back of the lobby to meet the "Great John L. Lewis," shaggy-browed president of the UMW.

"My heart was pounding," Dave recalls. "How thrilled I was. I couldn't believe this was happening to me, a kid not yet 21 years old. I was frightened. Lewis' personality was so overpowering. We shook hands. Then he gave me a big smile and said:

"Glad you're with us Dave, I wish you the best of success."

After meeting the Great John L., Dave was introduced to other mine leaders from the anthracite districts. They had just concluded an agreement with the mining industry and everyone was in high spirits.

It was hard to believe that all of these amazing things could happen at all—let alone be packed into the same day. Maybe he was still standing on the corner spinning daydreams?

The next night, Friday, Jack Dempsey and Luis Firpo, the "Wild Bull of the Pampas", were fighting for the world's heavyweight boxing crown in the Polo Grounds. Dave found he was floating on no fragile clouds, for that occasion.

Lewis, Murray and other UMW officials had tickets. They tried to get an extra one for Dave, but failed.

So, at four o'clock in the afternoon, he went out on his own to try to buy a ticket. He lined up on 154th Street two blocks from the ticket window in a crowd two abreast. The other side of the street soon filled and this mob rushed the double lines.

Dave discovered he was being swept along for a block without his feet touching the ground.

Mounted police threw up their boots in an effort to straighten the lines. Three hours later, with no sign of an opening, Dave resorted to the stratagems that had gotten him into Pitt Stadium and Forbes Field back in Pittsburgh. But there were too many cops to buck.

He then retreated to buy a hot dog. After seeing a riot develop around a little booth, he heard a wild report that $18 tickets were being sold for $5.00. So, he charged back into the mob.

"This is for me," he yelled.

It wasn't, though. A big guy propelled himself back from the booth with knees and arms flailing. Dave sailed back with him out of the crowd and couldn't fight his way through a second time.

At this point, police began swinging their heavy leather stirrups in an effort to get the crowd under control. Dave, feeling that discretion was the better part of valor, stayed on the outside, waiting a chance to advance again.

The chance came when a big, fat cop elbowed his way up to the booth. Dave clung right behind him.

Reaching the booth, the cop turned and asked:

51

"What do you want kid?"

"One of those tickets," Dave yelled.

The price advanced to $6.00 at this point. The battling steelworker from Pittsburgh shoved a handful of crumpled bills into the cage and was on his way into the Polo Grounds.

Inside, he found that the price of his seat entitled him to risk his neck straddling wooden benches. Everyone stood up once the fight got under way.

During a furious exchange, Dave landed on the floor.

"Who's down?" he screamed in the ear of a big Texan who reached down to help him up.

"You and Dempsey," the Texan roared.

Dave rode out the rest of the fight perched atop the Texan's shoulders. The crowd went mad when Dempsey hammered Firpo into a senseless pulp in the second round, to retain his title. Women cried. And young McDonald had his first taste of riot.

Saturday morning, the new secretary climbed on a train with mine officials bound for the hard coal fields. They got off at White Haven, Pennsylvania, where local mine leaders met them with a volley of cheers.

Frank Hughes was assigned by Murray "to take care of Dave and introduce him to the boys."

At the rally, from a seat in the stands, he heard Lewis and Murray in action for the first time. They made speeches about the new contract and hailed it as a great victory.

The miners were "so happy they were crying." The stands shook with their hard-booted stomping and applause. Then, they lined up to shake hands and embrace the officials.

It was an eye-filling initiation for the new secretary.

Dave hardly had recovered from the most exciting week of his life when Murray handed him his first big assignment, as secretary. Through it he learned that his duties were many and varied and usually called for fast action.

"We're going to Portland, Oregon, for the AFL convention," the UMW leader explained. "I want you to make all the travel arrangements."

For a fellow who had bought only an excursion ticket to Atlantic City, this was quite an assignment.

But the Greenfield boy did it with the help of an agent of the Pennsylvania Railroad. Tickets were bought for Mr. and Mrs. Murray, and Dave. The trip took them out on the Canadian Pacific through the Rockies, then by ship to Vancouver, British Columbia, to Seattle, and finally to Portland.

At the convention, Dave "sat away back in the hall where the miners always sat." This was his first ring-side view of a Commie fight. Also, the occasion of his introduction to Samuel Gompers, who presided, and William Green, who then was secretary of the UMW and chairman of the resolutions committee.

The Commie fight was a typical knockdown affair. One of the Red leaders, wearing a black shirt, led the battle

53

against an anti-Communist resolution introduced by Green.

United Mine Workers counterattacked by relating their experiences with the Reds in the mine fields. They told how the Reds tried to destroy the UMW in the 1919-22 strikes by lining up with the employers in an effort to break the strike.

Through it all, Dave observed that Gompers was a "dynamic little fellow who knew how to run the show."

On the trip, the new secretary worked in his spare time to polish up his shorthand. Murray was "very, very patient." He never forgot this side of his boss, and in later years he repaid this patience.

From Portland, the party moved on to San Francisco where they went sightseeing by auto. The last stop was Los Angeles for several days with Lewis and other UMW officials. Then, home on the Santa Fe.

Given a chance to settle into a regular routine, Secretary McDonald plunged into his job with the same drive he had displayed in learning every operation there was to know in the Hazelwood mill. He worked around the clock in an effort to get to know all of the UMW leaders.

At the same time, he was absorbing operations of the union and mining industry. He began a program of reading which made him exceptionally well-informed. But it wasn't long before he was on the move again.

CHAPTER 5

TOO MANY MINES AND TOO MANY MINERS

Not many young men in labor have embarked on a major collective bargaining conference at the age of twenty-one.

It happened to Dave McDonald in the winter of 1924, when the union began its fight for survival.

He attended the historic "Jacksonville Conference" of the United Mine Workers where the famous but ill-starred agreement was signed between the union and the Central Competitive operators on February 19, 1924. The agreement was to retain the $7.50 per day wage scale for five years.

Some thought it would be the formula for stabilizing the coal industry without government intervention. Among this group was the titan of the UMW, John Llewellyn Lewis, himself.

Lewis was quoted as exclaiming shortly after the signing: "Exactly as was foreseen by the United Mine Workers, the law of supply and demand is working a cure."

If the boss of the UMW was elated, it was not without cause. Up to that time, the mining industry had been driving hard to reduce the scale. New, low-cost machines were replacing men at the unionized pits, especially in the South. In Virginia, Kentucky, Tennessee and Alabama some diggers were working for as little as $3 a day and reportedly glad to be doing it.

This growth of non-union competition, especially in West Virginia and Kentucky mines which had been opened during World War I, poised the threat of cheap competition for the organized mines.

If getting the long-term agreement and retaining the wage scale now appears to have been both a surface victory and a stalemate, Dave McDonald differed not a bit from Lewis or Murray. He never even suspected it. Actually, to the happy UMW officials, it was equivalent to winning the Rose Bowl, or at least a Jacksonville, Fla., version.

On the train ride home, young McDonald celebrated with Patrick J. Fagan, president of UMW District 5 (Allegheny and Washington counties in the Pittsburgh area) and later city councilman in Pittsburgh; Bill Hargis, secretary-treasurer of the same district, and other members of their delegation.

Friendships were developed that lasted down through the years. He learned that "brother" is no idle salutation in the union movement.

Too Many Mines and Too Many Miners

In the Spring of 1924, Dave took another important step. He learned how to handle a convention by working with Oral L. "Olie" Garrison, secretary to Lewis, in making plans for the UMW convention in Indianapolis, Indiana.

For a first fling, he couldn't have picked a much tougher assignment.

It marked the first time that a public address system was used at any convention. Two microphones were set up, one for the chairman on the stage and the other down on the floor for the delegates.

This paved the way for more orderly convention procedure, eliminating the need for leather-lunged shouting and resulting sore throats.

But it didn't stop the bedlam at this session.

Frank Farrington, president of Illinois District 12, and Alex Howat, former president of Kansas District 14, rallied dissident factions and a large group of Communists in an intra-union battle against the Lewis-Murray leadership.

Communists and Socialists attempted to make a shambles of the convention. At a pre-arranged signal, 600 delegates charged down the aisles, threatening to take the platform by storm. Howat spurted down the middle aisle and scrambled over the press table to the platform.

Everyone in the hall stood up to see the action.

President Lewis, pounding a big gavel, attempted to restore order. But it was like trying to stop a typhoon with an oar.

Oddly enough, two minor figures stepped in to turn the tide. Bush McCormick, chief sergeant-at-arms, guarding the right side of the stage, grabbed Howat—first to make an assault on the stage—and hurled him back into the crowd.

On the left side, Whiskers Smith, an old Tennessee miner adorned with a flowing white beard, stood at the steps with a gun in each hand.

The unruly attackers knew he meant business. They stopped in their tracks.

John L. boomed out his defiance.

"May the chair state," he roared, "that you may shout until you meet each other in Hell and he will not change his ruling."

This was his refusal to give recognition to Howat and his previous instruction to the sergeant-at-arms to eject Powers Hapgood.

Periodically, there was derisive booing and a series of loud catcalls from the gallery, all of which Lewis chose to ignore until suddenly, he pointed to the location of the troublemaking Communists and thundered:

"Far too long there has lurked in that gallery the Arch-Prince of Communism in the United States who makes annual visits to Moscow to make his reports and receive his orders."

What happened to the offending Communist at this point can be left to conjecture. McDonald remembers

58

flying fists as several diggers indicated their disapproval of Communist etiquette in public places.

It was also at Indianapolis that McDonald learned some of the robust Lewis platform presence.

An unfriendly delegate would arise.

"For what purpose does the delegate arise?" would come the booming challenge from Lewis.

"I want to go on record," the troublemaker would begin.

"If you want to go on record, write it on a slip of paper and hand it in to the secretary. Next business."

So it went.

There was danger in the wings of that convention. But John L. Lewis was still boss.

For 10 straight days, Van A. Bittner, then chairman of the Resolutions Committee, stood up battling to put over the constitution.

The Commies howled, shouted, and blew whistles.

Finally, after countless bloody noses, black eyes and "busted heads," the constitution was adopted.

"All conventions since that one have seemed calm in comparison," Dave says.

That summer, Murray steamed off to the International Miners' Convention in Prague, Czechoslovakia.

Meanwhile, McDonald was assigned to work in the coal fields around Fairmont, West Virginia, with Van A. Bittner.

Here, Dave, as international representative in charge, received his baptism in organizing.

"I was really introduced to the rough, tough killer-gunmen type employed by West Virginia coal operators," he relates.

Camps resembled "prison stockades."

At meetings, he "looked down the muzzles of machine guns manned by Baldwin Felts detectives."

Every day, Dave would start out with a load of posters, box of tacks and hammer to advertise mass meetings called by the UMW. The posters were torn down almost as fast as they appeared.

It was a matter of doing the job all over again the next day.

Miners were beaten daily, and families evicted from their homes.

The UMW's work was largely a holding action, battling to halt encroachment of non-unionism.

"We considered it a successful day if one more mine didn't go non-union," Dave recalls.

At the end of that wild Summer, McDonald rejoined Murray in Pittsburgh. But there was no lull. They plunged into meetings and conferences leading up to the anthracite strike.

It took less than a year for every one of the elated group which had returned from the Jacksonville Conference to see how futile the agreement was. Coal, as an industry, showed two faces. In the bituminous or soft coal fields, there was "competitive throat-cutting."

Dominated by some 10 railroads, the hard coal or anthracite fields were ruled by unyielding monopoly.

Open repudiation of the Jacksonville Agreement came in July, 1925, from the Rockefeller-controlled Consolidation Coal Company which cut the wages of day men to $6.00. Others quickly followed through the breach in the wall. Next of these was the big Pittsburgh Coal Company which took action August 12th.

Of course, the lesser operators followed the lead. Union contracts were scrapped by operators in Pennsylvania, Northern West Virginia, and Ohio.

When the strike started, in the Fall of 1925, President Lewis decided to move his headquarters to Wilkes-Barre, Penna., so that he could direct it personally in the hard coal fields.

His secretary, Oral Garrison, was left at the permanent headquarters in Indianapolis. And Dave McDonald was called to Wilkes-Barre to work with Lewis as field secretary.

Dave no sooner had unpacked at the Redington Hotel than things began to break for a settlement. Lewis received a phone call from New York and, with the help of McDonald, slipped out right under the noses of a swarm of newspaper reporters.

According to the hastily-devised plan, Dave bought the

train ticket to New York, took Lewis' suitcase and met him on the platform as he climbed into the car.

"Just stay here and sit on the lid," Lewis told him. "Tell the press fairy tales until you hear from me."

Late in the evening "all hell broke loose."

Reporters discovered that Lewis was missing and couldn't find out where he had gone. They descended on McDonald en masse, angrily demanding to know where John L. was hiding out.

Throughout the night, they bombarded McDonald with questions and the phone rang incessantly. He told them "all sorts of fanciful things."

One widely-circulated story had Lewis "taking a walk in the woods with some New York financier."

When John L. learned of this report, his reaction, according to McDonald, was:

"I'll be God-dammed."

That was Dave's first engagement with the press and one of his toughest.

After settlement of the 1925 hard coal strike, the next big move for McDonald was to Miami, Florida, for the bituminous coal conference. No agreement could be reached. The coal operators asked the miners to take a wage cut. They refused, claiming that Pittsburgh Coal Company and Consolidated Coal Company of West Virginia (now Pittsburgh Consolidation Coal Company), two of the largest producers, had broken the "Jacksonville Agreement."

This led to the disastrous 1927 coal strike—one that dealt the UMW a shattering blow.

All of the Northern states went out. Embittered, tough times followed. The strike produced fighting and shooting.

Moving out into the bleak struck fields, Dave was in charge of assigning makeshift barracks to families evicted from their mine-patch homes by the companies. He worked with Murray and the energetic Pat Fagan, president of Pittsburgh District 5. This was Pittsburgh Coal territory. There were 17,000 miners and their families under the leadership of the lion-hearted Fagan. These represented the serried ranks of unionism, dropped from a proud 45,000 members in boom times.

"Women and kids were thrown out of their homes," Dave recalls bitterly. "It was a case of begging, borrowing money, clothing—anything we could get to take care of them. We built rough, pine board barracks to put something between them and the raw weather."

The strike dragged on hopelessly for 18 months and then expired gradually. When it ended the UMW was practically destroyed. Its nationwide membership had dwindled to 150,000 from a peak membership of 800,000 during World War I.

Although Lewis had sought in vain for help from Washington, no official voice or hand was raised to aid the stricken workers of the coal fields, save that of Senator Frank Gooding of Idaho, member of a subcommittee of the Senate Committee of Interstate Commerce.

As a matter of simple truth, the biggest public stir over the plight of the miners was over the propriety of the Senate group prying into conditions.

Senator Gooding made this stark comment:

"Conditions which exist in the strike-torn regions of the Pittsburgh District are a blotch upon American civilization. It is inconceivable that such squalor, misery and distress should be tolerated in the heart of one of the richest industrial centers in the world. The committee found men, women and children living in hovels which are more insanitary than a modern swinepen. They are breeding places of sickness and crime."

There was crime enough to come.

The senators had scarcely left the coal fields when two sadistic members of the "Coal and Iron" police murdered miner John Barkoski.

In a night-long orgy in their barracks they broke every bone in the body of the hapless Imperial, Pa., miner whose death was to prove the liberation of the coal fields from the oppression of these same "Coal and Iron" police.

The widow was paid $13,500 for the loss of her husband.

Said the district attorney: "It was the most brutal murder I have ever investigated."

Life in the coal fields had not yet caught up with civilization. Especially for union men and their families.

Dave's experiences in the terrible days of the 1925–27 strike in Western Pennsylvania was to have a particular value in connection with one of the most dramatic docu-

ments ever to come out of the coal fields of Pennsylvania—
the story *Black Fury* made into a motion picture by Warner Brothers with Paul Muni as the star.

Michael A. Musmanno, now Justice of the Supreme
Court of Pennsylvania, visited Philip Murray one day in
1934 with a large bundle of manuscript under his arm. It
was the novel which was to become *Black Fury.*

Musmanno asked Phil if he would look over the manuscript for suggestions or correction, for Phil knew the
saga of coal in all its vicissitudes, adventures, aspirations,
and ideals. Pointing to his young assistant, Dave McDonald,
Phil said:

"Mike, I have just the man to do the job. Dave Mc-
Donald not only knows coal mining, but with his genuine
interest in drama, he should be able to offer advice which
you may find very helpful."

McDonald read the manuscript and became a bonfire
of enthusiasm. He and Musmanno then went over the
story together, reliving the brutalities and atrocities of
Pennsylvania's Coal and Iron Police, the misery and the
squalor of the coal mining towns during the strike days,
the tyranny and oppression of coal operators.

This tragic episode was the realistic and dramatic foundation for *Black Fury,* and its searing unfoldment on
the screen did more than anything else to arouse the people
of Pennsylvania into a demand for the abolition of the
"Coal and Iron" police.

CHAPTER 6

THE ROOSEVELT ERA

Between the collapse of the 1927 coal strike and advent of the New Deal, the United Mine Workers of America crawled into a shell. More than $7,000,000 of union funds had been spent in trying to make the Jacksonville Agreement stick.

Union leaders could do little more than "hold the line" in a world seemingly populated with burnt-out slack piles and silent, rotting tipples.

Where his job as secretary had been spiced with danger and tumultuous activity, Dave McDonald now found it had become as dull as life in the gray, immobilized coal towns. By comparison with the fine frenzy in which he had been working, time weighed heavily on his hands.

So, to find an outlet for his excess energy, he turned to the stage. This was an old love and a natural outlet. Dave had taken more than a passing interest in the theater ever since reciting "Little Fishies in the Brook" from the counter of that Hazelwood butcher shop at the age of four.

He says now, with a rueful smile, "that butcher shop just naturally brought out the ham in me. I have never had the illusion that I am a frustrated Barrymore. My fondness for the theater and the enjoyment I get out of it—simply matches another man's liking for golf—or the next man's yen for fishing."

In high school he had frequently appeared in plays. His first role, ironically enough, was that of a bomb-throwing Bolshevik. That was about as far removed as he could get from the real-life role he was to play later as a vigorous anti-Communist labor leader.

Then, Father James Lavelle had lured him, in his late 'teens, to appear in a play at St. Roselia's Church.

It was almost inevitable that during the doldrum years of the UMW, his theatrical talents would emerge. With typical directness and enthusiasm, he enrolled in Carnegie Tech's drama school. Along with his acting and directing, for which he showed a genuine flare, he wrote one-act plays and produced others.

Feeling the need for more general education, he also took other night courses in English and Public Speaking.

Working on the direction and production of student shows at Tech gave him a "big kick." On the side, early in 1930, he teamed up with Richard Rauh and Morrie Fierst in helping organize the Pittsburgh Playhouse—a theater for amateurs. It eventually developed into a million-dollar project that gained nation-wide attention for Pittsburgh.

Dave seriously considered shifting from labor to the theater during this period. His work at Tech and at the Playhouse brought comment that encouraged him to go to Hollywood as a motion picture director.

Through State Senator Frank J. Harris, Pittsburgh theatrical mogul, came an opportunity to go to Hollywood with Warner Brothers as an assistant director. The job beckoned invitingly.

It was an opportunity almost too tempting to resist. The road to advancement with the United Mine Workers appeared to be filled with road blocks. And Dave was "awfully tired of just being secretary." As a young man of tremendous energies, equipped with lively ambition, he wanted action.

After picking up his certificate from Tech's drama department in 1932, Dave had just about made up his mind to take a fling at Hollywood. Some people were even pointing out that he could "work on either side of the camera," taking note of his good looks.

However, in November of that same year, Franklin Delano Roosevelt was elected President of the United States.

That changed the picture considerably and led, eventually, to the second "big break" of his labor career. He put Hollywood on the shelf to await developments.

After the nomination, Dave had gone with Murray and four other UMW officials to Albany, N.Y., to meet FDR—who then was Governor of New York, as well as the Democratic candidate.

Murray told FDR about the plight of the United Mine Workers. How they wanted a meeting with the soft coal operators so that a contract could be worked out—but the operators refused to meet.

After listening intently, FDR touched off an historic exchange with Murray, asking:

"What do you want me to do?"

"I'd like you to call a conference."

"All right, I'll do it."

"What if they don't come?"

FDR stuck out his jaw defiantly and reassured him:

"When I call them, they'll come."

The election of Roosevelt touched off a terrific UMW organizing campaign in the Spring of 1933. Although the union had only $125,000 in its treasury, John L. Lewis, Tom Kennedy, and Phil Murray decided to shoot the works in an effort to reorganize the mining industry.

The word to all non-union men was "The President wants you to join the union."

Springboard for this sweeping membership drive was Section 7 (a) of the National Industrial Recovery Act. Both Lewis and his chief counsel, Henry Warrum, interpreted this as the "right of labor to organize" clause.

Even the friendliest pro-union exponent of the NIRA

might have had difficulty in uncovering the legal sanction which Lewis saw here for his organizing drive. If the White House had made any pronouncement to this effect it had never reached the public.

Yet, John L. sent his apostles openly into territory where bloodshed would have greeted such efforts a short while before. They were armed with nothing more than the electrifying claim that "Your government says—'Join the United Mine Workers.' "

They joined.

McDonald recalls with great gusto that he and other officials "worked like mad that Spring."

Mass meetings drew crowds as large as 65,000. The hillsides were covered with men from the mines—trappers to pickmen. Thousands upon thousands of cards were signed. They were kept in show boxes in the offices of District 5 in Pittsburgh.

"Boy, did we sign 'em up," Dave chuckles, remembering the landslide results of the organizing efforts which were often conducted under the very noses of the dreaded coal and iron police. "So fabulous were the results of that drive," he remembers with evident pleasure, "that Lewis was as stunned as any of the non-union operators. We stormed in where even the hardiest legions of angels would once have feared to tread. By 1934 there were 400,000 organized miners."

The mine union was back in business, stronger than ever.

Living up to his pre-election promises, FDR called the mine operators and union officials together for a conference in Washington. The operators came, just as he said they would.

By that time, NIRA had been set up under General Hugh "Iron Pants" Johnson. Bargaining started at the Carlton Hotel on June 19, 1933, and lasted until September 22. McDonald worked with Van A. Bittner and Lewis in the stormy sessions at the Shoreham Hotel. Here he was treated to the incomparable performances of an ex-Cavalry General and the virile phrase-making of Lewis.

Although the somewhat demoralized operators had immediately responded to Roosevelt's call, most of them were privately of the opinion that this was but an interlude. The Supreme Court would make short work of the NIRA. The coal operators were "not there" in spirit. They provoked General Johnson to salty language by their reluctance to put anything on paper.

It was a gruelling three-month grind that seemed like an eternity. On many a night, McDonald worked long past midnight. He pounded a typewriter while others slept. Then had to be on the job again at 9 o'clock in the morning, with only a few hours sleep to reinforce him for the next day's work.

Every morning, he dashed from the Shoreham to the Carlton to pick up the mail and dig into the pile of stenographic work that accumulated during the night.

This went on continuously, seven days a week. There

were no days or nights, not an hour off to relax. Time just ran together in a jumble of one assignment piled on top of another.

One afternoon, McDonald and Bittner strode off to Goldhein's Men's Store to buy a couple of shirts. They were gone only for a few minutes when a searching party caught up with them in the store.

"They want you back at the hotel!" the lead searcher exclaimed.

Grabbing the shirts on the run, the shoppers beat it back to the Carlton Hotel.

There, an official voice asked:

"Where the hell have you and Bittner been?"

"Buying shirts—we wore out the old ones," McDonald explained, adding "we were only gone 15 minutes."

Going up to a meeting that already was in progress, Dave turned to Bittner and muttered:

"I'll be a son-of-a-bitch if this isn't awful. These guys act like they never heard of the 8-hour day or the 12-hour day either. They're working up to 24 hours, 7 days a week."

Before the conference ended, Dave's face matched the white walls of the meeting rooms. He hardly knew the sun was shining that Summer.

The only break, other than that shopping spree, came one night when he bumped into A. D. (Denny) Lewis, brother of John L.

"You're doing a nice job, kid," Denny remarked, clapping Dave on the back. "Let's take a walk and see if we can find a beer. You need a break."

They found a half-dozen beers and unwound.

The agreement, growing out of that conference, finally was signed on September 22, 1933, in the Pittsburgh Coal suite at the Shoreham.

Dave gave it its name—the famed "Appalachian Agreement." He wrote it in shorthand and typed it. He read it. He explained it at the climactic session. He also signed it, as assistant secretary.

The agreement, drawn up by Phil Murray and Charles O'Neil, chairman of the Central Pennsylvania Coal Operators Association and an ex-UMW official, established a $4 a day wage scale. During the "bust" years of the union after the disastrous 1927 strike, wages had fallen from $7.50 to $1.25 a day.

"It was pitiful," Dave says. "Miners came to the sessions in Washington in their pit boots and overalls. That's all they owned."

After the agreement was signed, Murray, Bittner and McDonald walked over into a corner of the room. They shook hands and wept unashamedly. They had carried most of the load. The relief of the signing was too great for them to have acted otherwise.

"We just couldn't help it," Dave explains. "It was the rebirth of the UMW."

Then, complete exhaustion set in.

The conference was the second "big break" for Mc-

Donald. The first came in hooking up with Murray after his friend Mark Stanton was unable to take the job of secretary 10 years earlier.

This conference projected him into the position of getting to know top men in the industry. He received many offers for better jobs and could have called his shot on salary.

However, he reasoned this way:

"No, I'm going to stay with the mine workers . . . I believe in this."

That same year his circle of acquaintances widened considerably. The more illustrious figures ranged from General "Iron Pants" Johnson, director of the NRA, to the then Monsignor Francis Haas, who 19 years later as Bishop of Grand Rapids, Michigan, delivered the eulogy at Philip Murray's funeral, shortly before his own death.

Along with having direct connections with the "perfectly mad NRA," he became an expert lobbyist.

The following year of 1934 he was back at the conference table. The first agreement had been for only six months. With Bill Hargis, he negotiated the "check-off" clause with the Western Pennsylvania Coal Operators Association.

This eventually became a model for the coal industry. And it was the first real personal negotiation for McDonald.

Meanwhile, the UMW added another feather to its hard hat by organizing the captive mines of the steel industry.

Then came the 1935 A. F. of L. convention in Atlantic

City jamming the Chelsea Hotel, where Dave played a life-saving role for John L. Lewis. It revolved around the furious fight over the principle of industrial versus craft unions. Lewis had decided that the time had come for action.

Charles P. Howard, the president of the Typographic Union and once a Kansas miner, had submitted a minority report urging immediate "organization of the unorganized."

Lewis followed with a speech that was both a declaration of policy and a challenge. In it he said, in part:

"The organization I represent has an interest in this question. Our people work in a great base industry, basic in its service to the American people and the economic and commercial processes of the nation. They struggle against great odds and against great influence, and the intensity of their struggle and the weight of their burden is greatly increased by reason of the fact that the American Federation of Labor has not organized the steel industry and a few other industries similarly situated.

"We are anxious to have collective bargaining in the steel industry and our interest in that is, to that degree, selfish because our people know that if the workers were organized in the steel industry and collective bargaining there were an actuality, it would remove the incentives of the great captains of industry to destroy and punish and harass our people who work in the captive coal mines throughout the country, owned by the steel industry."

75

UMW President Lewis, champion of industrial unionism, met head-on with Big Bill Hutcheson, head of the
carpenters' union at this juncture. During a torrid exchange over a point of order, Lewis said Hutcheson, who
packed 300 pounds on a six-foot-six frame, was "pretty
small potatoes." They approached each other like a couple
of Japanese wrestlers.

"You're nothing but a big, dirty bastard!" Hutcheson
raged.

Lewis resented this by promptly whopping his fist
against the bigger man's eye, ignoring the risk of a severe
beating from his oversized foe.

Before Big Bill could retaliate, McDonald, a wiry 185-
pounder, conditioned by handball and other strenuous
exercises, leaped upon Hutcheson.

Although Big Bill nearly doubled him in size, Dave
pinned him to the floor—employing an old friend-saving
trick he had mastered in numerous Greenfield street
brawls.

It took considerable time for A. F. of L. President
William Green to restore order. But the day had been
saved for Lewis, not to mention his features. And Mc-
Donald won his undying gratitude.

Out of that hectic convention emerged the Committee
for Industrial Organization. The next day, Lewis, Murray,
Thomas Kennedy, Sidney Hillman, David Dubinsky and
a few others met in the lounge of the President Hotel.

They decided then and there to form the CIO, which

later became the Congress of Industrial Organizations when the A. F. of L. kicked out the CIO unions.

After all, labor now had its "Magna Carta." The Wagner Act, signed July 5, 1935, recognized the rights of workers in well-defined terms. But it took a Supreme Court decision in 1939 to convince some segments of industry that the Wagner Act was not unconstitutional. For labor, "Independence Day" came on that 5th of July, 1935.

CHAPTER 7

REBIRTH OF THE STEEL WORKERS

On a sparkling Autumn day of 1935, the United Mine Workers of America were assembled in convention in Washington, D.C.

President John L. Lewis announced that the time had come to organize the steel industry. As delegates stomped and cheered the announcement, Dave McDonald strode across the stage to where Philip Murray was sitting and yelled:

"Well, here we go again, Boss!"

"What do you mean?" Murray asked.

Dave explained.

"It looks like you'll be put in charge of this organizing thing. Who else can do it?"

He was right. No one believed then, except possibly Lewis, that the steel industry actually could be organized after the abortive attempts of the previous quarter century.

The accomplishment of this feat is viewed by Murray-McDonald supporters as the "Miracle of the Union Age."

All that winter, top-level plans were laid for the organizing drive. On June 10, 1936, Dave rode home to Pittsburgh with Murray after one of the numerous conferences. As the train rolled by the blazing Braddock mills, Murray revealed his plans to make him secretary-treasurer of the Steelworkers Organizing Committee.

"That night I washed Hollywood out of my hair for good," McDonald says. The chance to enter the moving picture industry as an assistant director still dangled invitingly but he no longer was tempted to make the change.

Born and bred of steel, McDonald concluded that organization of the steelworkers was his destiny.

The next day, June 11, 1936, it was official: Philip Murray, Chairman, and McDonald, Secretary-treasurer of the SWOC.

Within a week, the Committee held its first meeting. Eleven carefully selected members met June 17, 1936, in the District 5 office on the 12th floor of the Commonwealth Building in Pittsburgh.

Along with Murray and McDonald, the group of mine union leaders and old-time steelworkers included: Van A. Bittner, Patrick T. Fagan, Lee Pressman, John Brophy, Clinton S. Golden, Leo Krzycki, Julius Hochman, Joseph Gaither and Thomas Gillis.

Launching of the SWOC, to Dave, was the "proudest and yet most challenging event" of his life.

79

Many of the heavy problems fell on his broad shoulders.

Prior to the first meeting, Murray and McDonald had met with the officers of the old Amalgamated Association—the defunct steelworkers' union which held the charter. It was the same union Dave's father fought and bled for.

Young McDonald wrote the agreement to take over the charter, pounded it out on a typewriter and gave the new organization its name SWOC. Both he and Murray signed the agreement.

June 17, 1936—the date of the first SWOC meeting—became founding day. It now is called "Phil Murray Day" and is celebrated annually with a dinner.

For operating funds, Lewis had sent a check for $25,000 payable to McDonald prior to the first meeting. But this was only a drop in the bucket. The SWOC couldn't really go into business until the UMW later kicked through with $500,000 for the organizing work. The loan eventually reached $601,000. And it wasn't until June 27, 1941, that McDonald could write the final $250,000 check to Thomas Kennedy, secretary-treasurer of the UMW, paying off the loan.

The financing details, alone, were enough to break the back of a weaker man than McDonald.

Fortunately, he found a sympathetic banker, Clarence W. Orwig, Vice-President of the Commonwealth Trust Company in Pittsburgh. Through him, he arranged for a checking account. After Dave explained that he would be writing the checks, they shook hands and Banker Orwig said:

"I wish you fellows success."

With these unexpected words of cheer, Dave scouted around for offices and finally settled on the 36th floor of the Grant Building. He explains:

"We picked the Grant Building for psychological purposes. It was the tallest building in downtown Pittsburgh. It was full of steel company offices. And we were on the top floor. We thought we would give the place tone and style."

The fortunes of the foundling union literally went up and down like the elevators serving that top-most floor in the Grant Building. But unlike the elevators, they eventually stayed up where their dreams had placed them.

Big Steel inadvertently opened the door for victory by the "outside union" as opposed to the favored Employee Representation Plan or company union.

Attacking the company unions on all fronts, the steelworkers celebrated Labor Day, September 7, 1936, with meetings in East Chicago, Canton, Massilon, Portsmouth, Steubenville, Johnstown and Pittsburgh.

Other gatherings were held with plenty of fanfare in New England, in the South and on the West Coast. Everywhere the spotlight was on one thing—demand for $5.00 a day. Big Steel came back with an open letter—refusing the demand on September 13th.

Phil Murray found a careless chink in Steel's armor,

and moved in for a rapier thrust at the weak spot in Steel's stated reasons for rejecting the demand. He argued:

"If it is just and fair to pay back dividends, why is it not just and fair to pay back wages? As your chart accompanying your letter shows, weekly earnings dropped 53.6 percent in June, 1932 from June, 1929. Don't you think it is just that these men who suffered such wage reductions in the dark years of the depression are entitled to the wages they lost in the same fashion as the stockholders are entitled to back dividends?"

Murray served notice that "the growing tide of the Steel Workers Organizing Committee campaign compels it a wage increase and the industry, with U.S. Steel leading, will grant it."

On November 6, the U.S. Steel Corporation announced pay increases to average 10 per cent and proposed that employe representation sign a wage agreement. This was something that Big Steel had fought since the beginning of the Twentieth Century.

Dave told Phil Murray, "We are breathing down their necks."

Today, he explains what happened with this comment:

"Once again the industry stumbled in its fight to stop unionization. Instead of a flat wage increase the proposal was made that it be tied to the cost of living. Before the hubbub of reaction died on that proposal, management was glad enough to forget the whole thing. Particularly, the proposal to sign an agreement."

82

Less than a year after the kick-off, the organizing drive paid a jackpot dividend. U.S. Steel Corporation signed an historic agreement on March 2, 1937, without a strike or any real resistance.

The news made headlines. When the union delegation was spotted walking into a Pittsburgh skyscraper, even newspapermen were excited.

There were reporters from all parts of the nation in the Steel City that day.

All were expecting strike news. Instead, they learned of a labor victory that was news in every capital of the world, in every city and crossroads village.

United States Steel had signed a contract with the Steelworkers Organizing Committee for a $5.00 a day minimum wage.

The Corporation agreed to recognize the SWOC for its members.

Yes, and it agreed to put the 40-hour week into effect with time-and-a-half for overtime.

Another major power, Jones and Laughlin Steel Corporation, fell into line and recognized the union after only a 36-hour strike.

But from there on, it was tough. Organizing reached the bitter stage with the "Little Steel Strike," revolving around the Inland, Republic, Bethlehem and Youngstown Sheet and Tube plants, later that same year of 1937.

Dave played a big role in that one. He averted a possible massacre in Youngstown, Ohio. The district director, near collapse from exhaustion and nervous tension, had lost control of the situation. McDonald rushed to the scene.

From his room high up in the Ohio Hotel, Dave looked out the window and saw three or four men poised with rifles on the roof of almost every nearby building. Learning that the Communists had organized a demonstration parade through downtown Youngstown that night, he quickly realized that this might produce the greatest massacre in union history.

Dave dashed over to union headquarters and called a meeting of all union leaders. Then, he read them the anti-riot act:

"I'm giving the orders. There will be no parade. And anyone who disobeys an order of mine will be fired on the spot. Now, get back to the picket lines where you belong. And I don't want to catch a single one of you in downtown Youngstown unless I send for you. This strike is not in the streets of Youngstown. Anyone who doesn't like it stand up now so that I can fire him."

No one stood up. And a possible massacre was averted.

However, the "Little Steel Strike," coming just as the SWOC began to crawl, nearly put the infant union out of business. The CIO was hard-pressed after its dramatic break with the A. F. of L., and had cut off funds. The new steelworkers' offspring had to stand on its own feet before it was able to walk.

Staff representatives were paid for only 14 days a month —or $84 and no expenses.

"What a great, loyal bunch of fellows they were," Dave says. "They stayed right in there with us through the lean years of 1937–38."

Another unsung hero in his book was George H. Cornelius, Jr., an Indianapolis, Ind., printer, who carried the SWOC on the cuff to the tune of $60,000. The printing firm went into hock grinding out the monthly dues buttons, pamphlets and other literature. It staked everything on the success of the steelworkers.

Dave would tell how tough things were with the steelworkers, that they had no money to pay the bills.

"That's all right," Cornelius would reassure him. "You boys are going to make it. I'll sweat it out."

McDonald has never forgotten this and frankly admits: "I don't see how we could have done it without Cornelius."

Still another key figure was M. C. Conick, of Main and Company. His advice and counsel in setting up the internal financial controls were "invaluable," according to McDonald.

In the wake of the 1938 recession, when the steel industry dropped to 14 per cent of capacity, the SWOC moved from the Grant Building into the Commonwealth Building to save rent. This was to become their permanent home. Their four-floor offices at 314 Fourth Avenue in Pittsburgh have been modernized with indirect lighting, air-conditioning and luxurious brown and green panelling similar to any other big business office.

85

Looking back, McDonald will tell you that 1937 was a history-making year. Its events changed history . . . for workingmen and their families all over America.

And it was a year that brought changes in Dave's personal life.

During the days when he was secretary of the SWOC and John L. Lewis was heading the Committee for Industrial Organization, Dave had met Emily Louise Price of Cleveland, Mr. Lewis' secretary.

They were married in that eventful year.

The late 1930s also brought additional duties. As the union grew, his responsibilities grew with it. Handling the housekeeping, the "G-3" or supply as it is known in the Army, McDonald built the internal organization on three firm foundations:

1. —Outside auditing.
2. —Internal controls.
3. —Full accounting of how every dues dollar was spent.

As Meyer Adelman, 450-pound district director in Milwaukee, summed it up:

"Phil Murray was the father and Dave McDonald was the mother of the CIO Steelworkers. Everyone who had a problem came and cried on Dave's shoulders."

Anytime a member had a baby or auto accident, it was Dave's personal problem. His organizing, collective bargaining and convention activities immediately became incidental, at least for the moment.

At times he thought he was "Mr. Fixit" to the world.

Early inspiration—his father, David J. McDonald and mother, Mary Kelly McDonald. Both parents were ardent supporters of the labor movement.

View of Hazlewood mill where Dave and his father worked—from roof of McDonald home, 1919. Both were out on strike that year.

Dave with kid brother Joe (left) and sister Peg in the Greenfield days.

Signing papers as Secretary-Treasurer of the SWOC, 1937.

Discussing Taft-Hartley Act changes with then Secretary of Labor Martin Durkin (in dark suit, seated at center). McDonald is seated, second from left; John L. Lewis stands at extreme right.

Mapping post-war strategy for the Steelworkers, 1945. L. to R. Clinton S. Golden, McDonald, Philip Murray and Van A. Bittner.

They were mum awaiting recommendation of President's fact-finding board on steel wage boost in 1949. Around table, Walter Reuther, McDonald and Phil Murray.

McDonald (extreme left) with Sherman H. Dalrymple, President, United Rubber Workers, and Lt. General George S. Patton, Jr., head group of labor leaders inspecting European warfront, August 1944.

After signing 1953 contract with Jones & Laughlin Steel Corp., McDonald exchanges customary shake with J. & L.'s W. R. Elliott. Looking on is USA Secretary-Treasurer I. W. Abel.

Check for $250,000 gift to Truman Library, Grandview, Mo., is turned over to Chairman Basil O'Connor. Making presentation for CIO Executive Board (in group) are James B. Carey, McDonald and Walter Reuther.

McDonald and Murray, seeming grim and intense, listen to speech of President Truman during 1952 steel strike.

Death of Murray in 1953 saddens trio of associates—James Carey, James Thimmes and McDonald.

Man of steel at his desk in the union's Pittsburgh headquarters.

Sailing to Europe in 1953 with his wife, Rosemary, and his son, Dave, Jr.

Dave and Rosemary with William Steinberg, conductor of the Pittsburgh Symphony Orchestra.

Taking oath as Steelworkers' President from Evan (Buck) Jones.

On Atlantic City boardwalk in 1953, McDonald strolls with George Craig, Philadelphia CIO regional director (left), and Nordy Hoffman (right).

Signing 1953 contract with U. S. Steel's John A. Stephens.

Both Stephens and McDonald seem happy after affixing signatures.

Dave seems less than jovial at this meeting with President Eisenhower whom the Steelworkers opposed in 1952. The late Alan Haywood shakes hands with Ike. Walter Reuther is between them. McDonald and James P. Carey, wear polite smiles, at right.

McDonald (center) stands next to Democratic candidate Adlai Stevenson at this pre-election meeting in New York City, 1952.

After death of Murray, McDonald makes report to 1952 CIO convention in Atlantic City. Photo of Murray occupies place of honor.

At "McDonald Day" dinner in Pittsburgh, November 28, 1953, honored guest, with Robert F. Wagner, Jr. (left), New York's Mayor-elect, and General Chairman William J. Hart, USA District 19 Director.

Touring plants with U. S. Steel's Benjamin F. Fairless, right.

Four studies . . . persuasive . . . attentive . . . thoughtful . . . forceful.

CHAPTER 8

TAKING OVER FOR MURRAY

Not until the Pearl Harbor year of 1941 did the steelworkers finally get their organizing drive over the hump. In a sense, this was history repeating itself. Great strides had been made by labor during World War I, only to be lost in the years that followed.

But this time there was a difference—a big difference.

The second SWOC convention, in the Morrison Hotel, Chicago, May 14th to 17th, 1940, had showed 654 companies under contract, and 823 lodges functioning and represented. Between the SWOC and a clean sweep lay "Little Steel."

As McDonald observed, "the slow, legal processes before government agencies, involving all these companies, bared their company-unions for what they were, and pointed the finger at them for the strikes of 1937.

"We were determined that, before the third convention

87

of the union was called to order in 1942, we would be able to report success on all fronts."

At this critical point, SWOC leader Philip Murray suffered a heart attack. He was sidelined for more than a year. It was his second serious illness, coming after a similar attack in 1937. Murray had shouldered new burdens when he had taken over as president of the CIO, not too long back.

This, of course, was when John L. Lewis resigned the post, true to his famous pledge as he went on record opposing Roosevelt's third term in 1940:

"It (re-election with the support of labor) will mean that the members of the Congress of Industrial Organizations have rejected my advice and recommendations," he had declared. "I will accept the result as being the equivalent of a vote of no confidence and will retire as President of the Congress of Industrial Organizations in November."

So, along with his regular organizing, day-by-day financial affairs, and convention work, Secretary-Treasurer Dave McDonald stepped into the breach and took over the heavy administrative duties during Murray's illness in 1941.

He smoothed off the rough edges of "Big Steel," completed the organization of "Little Steel" and handled the contract negotiating conferences with Bethlehem, Republic, Youngstown and Inland Steel companies.

None of this could be called an off-hand accomplishment. Nor were the results, by any means, due to McDonald's efforts alone.

88

It was a sizable assignment, accomplished with finesse. Perhaps it was the actor, rising to a great role; or merely the maturity of a man who knew both labor's goal and steel's history, and was, therefore, determined that the final skirmish must redeem all the lost battles.

The details of the fighting are to be found in the record. For example, Youngstown Sheet and Tube capitulated on March 29, 1941. Or to put it more exactly, the company entered into a stipulation with the SWOC and the National Labor Relations Board to reinstate those strikers who had been discriminated against and pay back wages amounting to more than $170,000. It also provided for what the union's public relations director called "final burial for the company-union."

So it went, too, with Republic where ghosts of the Memorial Day Massacre might well have found some recompense for their lives to see five thousand strikers restored to their jobs with back pay of a half-million dollars.

What was really accomplished in these final victories in the bitter citadels of "Little Steel" was expressed by a card-carrying member:

"What I like is being able to walk down the main street of town and talk to anybody I like about anything I like."

That simple pleasure was hard bought.

Besides those killed on Memorial Day, six other members lost their lives on picket lines, three in Massillon, two at Youngstown, one in Beaver Falls, Penna. These outbreaks occurred at half a dozen mills; hired trouble-

89

makers were in the field; scores were injured by tear gas and clubs.

Getting these agreements with "Little Steel" meant carrying case after case before the National Labor Relations Board. Dave came through with important "check-off" and maintenance of membership concessions.

Dr. Frank Graham's NLRB opinion, establishing the check-off system, quoted directly from McDonald's arguments that had been presented at the sessions in Room 726 of the Carlton Hotel in Washington, D.C.

Not only were Dave's conclusions accepted by the NLRB, but his language as well.

The "check-off" system of the company taking membership dues from the payroll of those workers who agree, and then paying the money to the union, was a key step in the growth of the Steelworkers and other major unions. It unlocked the door to huge memberships.

During this period, under the leadership of McDonald and with the momentum of the early organizing years, the Steelworkers made their greatest membership gains.

Dave had passed a back-breaking test and gained considerably in stature by the time Murray was able to return to his regular duties in 1942.

That same year, the United Steelworkers hatched into a full-fledged international union of the CIO. McDonald formally was elected secretary-treasurer of the new union. He served in this role until the death of Murray.

The union's graduation exercises were more than just formalities.

It is easy to understand why.

Picture yourself in the great Public Music Hall of the Cleveland Auditorium.

It is May 19, 1942.

A motion to adopt the partial report read by Clinton S. Golden, chairman of the Committee on Constitution, has just been carried unanimously.

The motion provided:

". . . This organization shall be known as the United Steelworkers of America, hereinafter also referred to as the International Union.

"This International Union shall be affiliated with the Congress of Industrial Organizations."

Chairman Philip Murray remarked, simply:

"Well, there you are. Beginning with this afternoon you start out as members of the United Steelworkers of America."

The hour was 12:30 P.M.

It was High Noon, indeed.

"It was the greatest thing that could have happened," Dave says. His only regret was that his father, who died in 1932, didn't live to see it. His mother, though, not only was on the scene, but lived to see the union grow far beyond her fondest dreams before she passed away in 1945.

During the early war years, in the feverish rush to turn

out defense materials, the affairs of the union and its relationship with employers ran a smoother course. The demands on him as secretary-treasurer lessened and Dave turned to new fields.

As secretary of the CIO's Political Action Committee in 1943, he helped raise millions of dollars. The PAC, a unique venture, gave labor a lusty voice in politics—although it is still hard to measure the effect. Dave advanced to the executive board and eventually, in 1949, to head PAC man for the steelworkers.

His position as labor leader also was enhanced on being elected in 1943 to the Presidency of the Steel City Industrial Union Council. This is the central delegate body of Pittsburgh district CIO unions. Dave was unopposed, succeeding Pat Fagan, President of UMW District 5, who resigned when John L. Lewis marched the miners out of the CIO in one of his famous huffs.

In addition to his USA duties, Dave served on the CIO executive board, and as a member of the housing, social security, Latin American affairs and other committees. As secretary of the CIO Southern Organizing Committee, he drew the blueprint for the Dixieland drive.

The Yankee organizers discovered the South was still anti-union.

Pick your town, it made little difference.

One man remembers with wry humor:

"I was ridden out of town on a rail. That's not luxury travel. They threatened me with instant death if I returned. What's more, they meant it. I'd had a taste of their temper. Yes, I was lucky. Looking at those shacks they called home, backward towns, god-forsaken hills, clay fields, and sandy loam roads, I decided I was a hell of a lot luckier than any of them. Anybody living like they were should have been out with invitations for union organizers."

But, there was only one standing invitation for those men who came down to spread the union gospel, and to preach relief for the misery and destitution everywhere to be seen in the storybook land of cotton: "Get out!"

Here's how the men who were down there talk about it:

"Nobody waited for nightfall in Gadsden, Alabama. This was the Iwo Jima of all the Dixie towns. Just let somebody discover you had a union emblem on you. Town toughs joined the company thugs and beat you free of charge. Right in the business district in broad daylight.

"The anti-union line was held in Gadsden with all the power and wealth of Republic Steel behind it. And Republic had company; Goodyear Tire and Rubber and others rallied against all strangers bearing the union message. Nor were they kindly to their own citizens who embraced the alien doctrine. Steel company police carried sidearms, nasty tempers and itchy fingers through the streets, night and day.

"There were few good Samaritans to pour oil and bind up the horribly-beaten unionists found by the wayside many cold, gray mornings after being waylaid at night. To the everlasting credit of these stout-hearted men, the union organizers stayed. They stayed despite violence and at the risk of personal safety.

"You came back to your office and found it a shambles, with smashed windows and furniture, and a viciously-worded note telling you to get out—*pronto*.

"When you failed to go, they moved in at night. Suddenly you found your teeth smashed, then the body beating began. It took place after a short ride to the edge of town. You could hear a roaring in your ears and might think, perhaps, you were losing consciousness already . . . But the sound of falling water turns out to be real. A swift stream arches over a precipice and drops sixty-five feet to swirl and boil below. The bruisers hold you over the brink.

" 'See that, you union bastard?' they demand.

"They thump the 'yes' out if you are short of breath.

" 'Next time, over you go.'

"With that your hosts are gone.

"Some men who were hard to convince were found downstream. They still wore their union emblem. Southern hospitality forbade stripping a doomed man.

"But the SWOC refused to give up."

Courage of this high order fanned a spark into a flame. First sign of a change came in that long-remembered year.

Resistance faded away. Even Gadsden, Alabama, became free—at last.

In the fall of 1943, Dave was off to South America in the interest of increasing production vitally needed for the defense effort. Talks to workers, government officials and employers launched him as an international labor leader. No labor man today has had more experience in the international field.

On his five-week tour of South and Latin American countries, he learned, much to his surprise, that labor movements had been operating on the lower continent as long as those in the United States. However, there was a vast difference in the workers' status. It boiled down to a single word—"opportunity."

"Workers down there," he explained on returning, "must combat class distinctions which are very difficult to surmount. In most South American countries, a man is an obrero—a member of the workers group; an empleado—which means a technician or white-collar worker; or a padron—an employer.

"They are born into those groups, and it is hard to break down the class distinction.

"There is little chance for education beyond a few grades and a man stays for life in his group. In the United States, however, the only thing to limit a man is his own brain power and drive."

With other labor leaders, he visited Chile, Peru, the Canal Zone, Panama, Colombia, Cuba and Mexico, representing the Office of the Co-ordinator of Latin American Affairs, headed by Nelson Rockefeller.

On this good will tour, he found that the United States "has real friends down there, from government leaders to the obreros on the lowest rung of the economic ladder." A sharp student of detail and quick to size up any new situation, Dave discovered strong labor organizations in many places:

"In Chile, 300,000 of the 1,000,000 employees were organized with widespread collective bargaining. Their labor movement was fully as old as ours. In Peru, the movement was embryonic. In Colombia, it was about 10 years old, but the transportation workers on the Magdalena River had a strong union of 27,000 workers.

"Panama's labor movement was just beginning, but Cuba had powerful unions, with perhaps 350,000 of 1,125,-000 employables organized. In Mexico, labor was strong—both the Confederatione Trajabadores de Mexico and the independents. Both the CIO and A. F. of L. were active."

Although living standards and working conditions in many South American nations fell far short of United States standards, McDonald had this forward outlook:

"It's a land of the future. And the workers down there will have improved conditions as they go along. The unions certainly are friends of this country and in several nations, they were quite largely responsible for their governments breaking ties with the Axis."

Continuing his travels, Dave plugged the "Good Neighbor" policy in Canada, Mexico and Cuba.

In August 1944, he ploughed across the Atlantic into the

battlefields of France with five other labor leaders. Accompanying him on this tour were R. J. Thomas, president of the United Auto Workers, and Sherman Dalrymple, president of the Rubber Workers Union, selected, along with McDonald by CIO President Murray; Frank P. Fenton, director of organization for the A. F. of L., A. L. Wegener, Assistant to President Edward J. Brown of the Electrical Workers Union, and Eric Peterson, Vice-President of the International Association of Machinists, representatives of A. F. of L. President William Green.

The labor battalion went over to see in action the equipment which U.S. industry and labor were grinding out at a record rate.

Along with other members of the party, Dave met General Dwight D. Eisenhower who later was to become President of the United States. They dropped in for lunch with "Ike" on August 22, 1944, at Supreme Headquarters Advance Command Post. Two other luncheon guests at the table that day were Lt. General Omar N. Bradley, head of the U.S. 12th Army Group, and Lt. General H. C. Lee, Commander of the Communications Zone.

During the tour of the battlefront, McDonald heard that GI's were concerned about the rumor that their old jobs wouldn't be there for them when they returned home. This was a subject on which he could give them quick and unequivocal assurance.

Dave told them that, while the Selective Service Law "doesn't say what it is supposed to say about jobs being

97

there for servicemen when they return," the CIO had insisted on getting this guarantee in its contracts.

He told them that 300,000 Auto Workers and 200,000 Steelworkers in service were being carried on union rolls in good standing without paying dues; and promised that no initiation fees would be required when they were mustered out of service and returned to their jobs. This reassuring news scored quite a hit with the troops.

With the sights and sounds of the battle for Normandy making a deep impression on him, Dave returned to Pittsburgh with this message for the home front:

"You've done a swell job. Now finish it."

Nowhere had he found the drive slowed down for lack of supplies, although the troops, at times, were close to running short. However, a General warned that it was "like rescuing a man from a well—if you don't pull him up the final few feet, you might as well have let him stay at the bottom of the well."

Dave was especially impressed with the tremendous job being done by the Services of Supply troops. With a sharp eye for detail, he found many examples of their Yankee ingenuity.

To win the battle of the "hedge-rows" in Normandy, they fashioned plows of abandoned German steel, hooked them to the front ends of tanks and ripped through overgrown embankments that had served as German fortifications.

Many German tanks were destroyed by igniting their

spare gasoline tanks with incendiary bullets and home-made "Molotov Cocktails."

Assembly lines—for trucks, jeeps and equipment—operated in open fields not too far from the front. Repair depots everywhere speedily put damaged equipment back into service.

In relating these incidents told to him by GI's, McDonald concluded that:

"Many of the inventions came from the minds of ordinary soldiers, but the General Staff, too, has displayed imagination in its conduct of the invasion."

When the invasion was being assembled, English roads were marked with U.S. highway signs made of metal from damaged oil drums. A certain unit was told to follow U.S. 30 to the port of embarkation, then pick it up on the other side and follow it on to Berlin.

"It was a great morale builder," he concluded.

During the 18-day tour, largely by plane covering 12,000 miles, McDonald travelled so close to the front that he frequently had to hit the ditches. The party visited hospitals in the forward area, talked to boys on stretchers, saw thousands of little white crosses and French people trying courageously to make a new start in their shattered homes and farms.

It left Dave with a hatred for war that has made him an active campaigner for world peace through the advancement of international labor unionism.

At the close of World War II, McDonald helped form

99

the World Federation of Trade Unions in 1945 at San Francisco when the United Nations was organized.

Five years later, after the WFTU fell into the hands of the Communists, he helped wreck it—and install in its place the International Confederation of Trade Unions. The groundwork for the new organization was laid in London in the Fall of 1949.

Another trip in 1945 took him to the Chapultepec Conference in an advisory role.

Two years later, in 1947, McDonald crossed the Atlantic again to work with the steel unions in England. He became well known in labor circles on the continent, conferring with union and government officials in France and Italy.

His many international ties included membership on the steel committee of the International Labor Organization, a branch of the United Nations, and on the ERP labor advisory committee in 1948.

It was in 1950 that Dave was asked to review the milestones which the great Steelworkers union had passed so swiftly. In a network radio address he told of the final victory for the men of steel; the swift completion of a journey—no, a crusade to unionize the nation's basic industry.

His mother, Mary Kelly McDonald, and sternly unionized father must have been listening and enjoying every word of it, somewhere in the great outer spaces into which his rich voice was cast. Perhaps a phrase or two sounded

100

familiar even in Heaven. This is what he said in recounting the Steelworkers' Odyssey:

"Unionization of the gigantic steel industry, beginning in 1936, was, virtually, the accomplishment of the impossible. True, many other mass-production industries were likewise organized during this period, but the background of opposition to unions, therein, was in no measure comparable to the historic opposition of steel owners to legitimate organization.

"Then, too, a nation encouraged to organize through the New Deal policies of President Franklin D. Roosevelt, beginning in the early 30's, focused its attention on the campaign in steel.

"There is a saying in the United States that as steel goes so goes the Nation. This is a measure of the condition of our economy. Likewise, in a sense, as the steel union campaign went so would go many other campaigns.

"All too widespread was the belief that steel could never be organized. This conviction was not without a record to substantiate it. When the steel industry, in the Homestead strike of 1892, began what later proved to be a fight to destroy unionism, the then union in steel, the Amalgamated Association of Iron, Steel and Tin Workers, started on the path to oblivion.

"Subsequent defeats on the picket line in 1901, 1910, and particularly in 1919, lent credence to the belief that steel, indeed, would never be organized! Yet, the seemingly im-

101

possible was to be accomplished before the middle of the century.

"It is not necessary to recall the organizing mistakes made by labor, other than to point out that the key to success was entirely overlooked by those in charge of earlier union campaigns. This was simply the fact that the *craft* unit, suitable in many cases, was entirely unsuited to mass-production industries. A new form was needed.

"Actually, it was not necessary to formulate any new idea in union format. In coal mining and the needle trades *industrial* unions had proved their worth. These industrial unions were strong and militant and brought together all workmen, from the common laborer to the highest skilled, in one union. The American Federation of Labor and the Amalgamated Association knew this but were loath to change their policies.

"It was this hesitancy on the part of the Amalgamated, as much as company opposition, which caused an overnight growth to approximately 200,000 in the early New Deal days, to dwindle to about 8,000 when the new campaign began in 1936. The Amalgamated concerned itself almost solely with the 'aristocrats' of the steel industry, namely, skilled rollers, puddlers, and the like. The great mass of workers were virtually ignored.

"Again, the unyielding attitude of the A. F. of L. toward industrial unionism brought about the creation of the CIO, the Congress of Industrial Organizations, when the A. F. of L. expelled its adherent unions.

"Six million *new* union members (the CIO membership) belie the supposed tragedy in the house of American Labor, regrettable as that division is.

"Under the brilliant guidance of Philip Murray, president of our Union and the CIO, the impregnable steel industry was unionized in the decade of 1936–1946.

"But it was no easy task and men gave their lives for the cause. Because of the open sentiment for unionism, in its far-flung operations, United States Steel Corporation signed an agreement within a year, with the union.

"But some of the so-called 'Little Steel'[1] companies, their mills loaded with guns, ammunition and tear gas, chose war. The 'Little Steel' strike of 1937 resulted. Twelve men lost their lives and scores were wounded. While the strike did not result in immediate victory, by 1941–1942 all the 'Little Steel' companies had recognized the union.

"Likewise, collective bargaining was not always successful at the conference table. In 1946 the union called a nationwide strike in steel to improve wages—and won.

"Briefly, then, in the first ten years of its existence the United Steelworkers of America grew to a membership of 900,000; won vacations with pay; overtime pay after eight hours a day and 40 hours a week; premium pay for late afternoon and night shifts—and boosted wages from an average of 66 cents an hour in 1936 to $1.31 an hour!

"This background is given because I felt it would be

[1] The term "Little Steel" is a loose designation of steel companies other than United States Steel which is colloquially called "Big Steel."

helpful in understanding the continuing progress of our union in the period 1947 to 1950 inclusive, about which I have been asked specifically to report.

"Entrenched as it was by 1946, the union did not rest on its record but continued to push organization—as it does even today—so that by the middle of the century it had reached a membership of one million in basic steel, fabricating, aluminum and more recently, the non-ferrous mines and mills—the latter jurisdiction having been given to the United Steelworkers of America after the expulsion of eleven unions by the CIO because they were Communist dominated.

"Our union has been universally known to be free from the stigma of Communist influence, but delegates to the 1948 convention decided to make certain that it would stay that way. The convention wrote into its Constitution a provision barring Communists and fellow-travelers from holding any office in the union.

"Nor was our union content with that amazing gain in wage rates. It adopted a new wage policy demand in April, 1947, signed a two-year contract which won an additional 15-cents an hour increase. Again in July, 1948, the union negotiated another wage increase—an average of 13 cents an hour! In 1949 the union, after a month's strike, negotiated a contract which won a minimum $100 a month pension [2] paid for entirely by the companies, and social in-

[2] The pension is actually figured on years of employment and average pay, but all workers are guaranteed a minimum of $100 a month, if they are age 65 and have 25 years service. Included in the pension is the

104

surance to provide medical and hospital care which is jointly paid for by the companies and the workers. In 1950, the union again opened its contract and won an average 16 cents an hour increase.

"Thus, the average hourly wage rate in the steel industry is now about $1.90—a true tribute to the economic strength of unionism when it is realized that the 1936 average was 66 cents an hour!

"Important as is the pay envelope of the worker, it must not be assumed that the United Steelworkers of America restricts its objectives to that alone. The growth in stature of the union would naturally make it a force to be reckoned with in other activities. As a matter of policy, the union overlooks no opportunity to be of help to communities and the Nation. And it is recognized as a potent organization everywhere.

"In more than 100 steel centers, homes built by local unions are the center of social activities. Free moving pictures for children are a regular Saturday morning entertainment. Social and fraternal groups of all kinds center their activities in union halls. Many of the halls are equipped with gymnasiums.

"A broad education program which uses the facilities of some 15 colleges and universities for summer courses equip the steel worker to be better union men and better

---

amount paid by the United States Government's Social Security Pension Plan.

105

citizens. Community relations are emphasized in these courses.

"Union members are taking their rightful place in public office, in charitable campaigns—in brief, in every activity which is helpful to communities. Our union is represented on the top-most level in nearly every Community Chest in the Nation. The Community Chest is the medium for raising funds annually for worthy charitable and social organizations.

"Our union now has in operation a vast athletic program with thousands of members participating in every type of sport activity in our country. Many of our members have gone on to become champion performers in baseball, football, basketball. In fact, the national ski-jump record is held by a member of the United Steelworkers of America.

"In the legislative halls of our national Congress and in state legislatures we have spokesmen who present the union's position on pending legislation to these public servants. We have developed a detailed program of political activity in support of candidates, in arousing interest in elections, in aiding members to register and in seeing that they vote on election days.

"Each member of our union is kept abreast of policy through our official publication *Steel Labor* which is mailed to the home. This is supplemented by letters to local union officers and by distribution of millions of pamphlets annually. This holds true, also for related national and international problems. Our union was among the champions of the so-called Marshall Plan for aid to Europe.

"The United Steelworkers of America speaks forth on all important problems. Its position is never in doubt.

"Success has attended the efforts of our union but we always keep before us these few words of caution from President Murray:

" 'While we may be carried along on the spirit of victory, let us not be lulled into any false sense of security.

" 'A powerful union is still the most important factor in the economic life of our people. Our every act must be aimed toward making this union an ever more effective weapon in fighting the battles of the working people of America.' "

This was a man who spoke with pride—and a firmly unshakable belief in the essential righteousness of Labor's cause.

McDonald was a dedicated man.

Listening to his radio summary of the long road which the men of steel had travelled, a craneman turned to his wife and said:

"That's a steel worker talking."

CHAPTER 9

THE NEW PRESIDENT

Heavy clouds hung over the top 17th floor of Hotel William Penn. It was a day of grave decision for the Steelworkers.

Waiting for the meeting to begin, a few men stood apart, talking quietly. Others watched the sparse Saturday morning traffic in the narrow streets below.

The somber weather that had moved over Pittsburgh's Golden Triangle during the night matched the mood in the room.

Grim-faced members of the executive board of the CIO United Steelworkers had a job to do. They were met on a solemn occasion. The date was Saturday, November 15, 1952.

For the first time in the union's history, the President's chair was empty. Philip Murray had died suddenly the previous Sunday in San Francisco and had been laid

108

tenderly to rest in Castle Shannon near Pittsburgh on Thursday.

A mild, unseasonable rain began to streak the windows as the men took their places.

For a moment there was a hushed waiting. Then the group at the conference table turned to the man who had helped launch the unionization of steel. Dave McDonald had been the personal choice of Philip Murray as his right arm in the battle against "the sleeping giant" of unorganized steel. Now, he was again chosen, this time to lead the great union which he had helped to create.

With the full backing of the executive board, the union's loyal and long-time secretary-treasurer who had grown up with the labor movement moved into the empty chair.

He was chosen "acting" President of the giant million-member union. Later, on February 10, 1953, he would be formally elected to a four-year term at the regular referendum election.

Dave's elevation to the Presidency came as he approached his fiftieth birthday, the following Saturday. It was a mighty challenge—the climax of 30 years of hard work with the United Mine Workers, United Steelworkers and parent CIO in almost every field.

If, as has been rumored from time to time, his warm, three-decade association with Philip Murray had cooled in the late years, there was nothing in McDonald's attitude to give such rumors substance. His words were vibrant with feeling when he spoke.

109

"I am most humble," the silverhaired labor statesman told newspaper reporters.

"I shall miss Philip Murray as much, if not more than any other man. I hope that Almighty God will give me the wisdom to carry on as I know he would want me to carry on.

"I shall direct every bit of energy that I possess to further the interests of the United Steelworkers of America and the working men and women of our country.

"This is a great country. And it shall always be my purpose to try to help to make it greater, not only for the people of America, but for all the people in the world."

I. W. Abel, 44-year-old director of the Canton, Ohio, District, succeeded McDonald as Secretary-Treasurer. James G. Thimmes was re-elected International Vice-President.

The executive board passed a resolution paying tribute to Murray. It read:

"America and the world are poorer today than they were just six short days ago. They have lost a great man, a man who contributed much and who, if he had lived, would have contributed more to all of the larger communities of which we are a part.

"We, in this room, feel that no one can know the extent of our loss and our grief. But the greatness of Phil Murray was that this same feeling exists in the hearts of millions of men. We have lost the father of our union.

"Other unions have had leaders—great and inspiring

leaders and . . . there must always come a time when those leaders are lost to them . . . but none, we think, can lose not only a leader, but one who bore such a close and personal relationship with all of those who served him and who he served all through his life.

"Philip Murray loved us. And we loved him.

"Philip Murray is not dead so long as the things which he built continue to live. The CIO and all the other organizations and causes to which he gave so much will continue to keep his memory bright by working and building the things which he built and helped to build."

One of President McDonald's first acts was to announce that the union had been approached by the Pittsburgh Junior Chamber of Commerce, which 10 years earlier had given its first "Man of the Year" award to Murray. The Chamber proposed to set up a permanent, annual "Philip Murray Award." McDonald gave the project his full backing.

A few months later, Dave walked into the headquarters of South Side Local 1272 on Sarah Street to cast his ballot. He was a candidate without opposition. It was mild for February 10th and the newspapers were marvelling at the 45 degrees. Some 54 years before, the *Pittsburgh Press* reported, the city had been paralyzed with a 20-below-zero cold spell.

Dave noted too, in the paper he had left on the seat of his car, that former Senator David Aiken Reed had died at Sarasota, Florida. He remembered that Reed had a rep-

111

utation amounting to genius for his analysis and presentation of technical data in court cases. He could admire that talent in any man, having always set great store by full records, well cited in negotiations.

He was touched by the warmth and sincerity of the men he had encountered in the local headquarters. These men would never know how much their loyalty and friendship meant, he mused. He must never, under any circumstance, fail them, he told himself.

The referendum election swept McDonald into office with 294,244 votes and no opposition. He was sworn in March 11, 1953.

In a stirring 66-minute inaugural address, he told an audience of more than 800 district directors and members of the union's staff attending ceremonies in the Hotel William Penn Ballroom:

"To the utmost of my ability and with the help of Almighty God I shall administer the office of President of the United Steelworkers of America honestly, fearlessly and devotedly. . . .

"I can fill the unexpired term of Philip Murray, but I cannot fill the role of Philip Murray. I assure you I will fill it so far as is humanly possible exactly as he would have filled it."

Turning to the ground-breaking ceremonies at Jones and Laughlin's South Side plant earlier in the week, Dave cited this as an indication that the union and steel industry are developing a degree of cooperation that never existed before. He pointed out that Evan (Buck) Jones, Local 1272 President, and Admiral Ben Moreell, Jones and Laughlin Board Chairman, exchanged pledges of mutual respect and confidence.

This was an unprecedented gesture of goodwill.

Although much had been accomplished, President McDonald told the district directors that he felt there were new goals to be won—that both progress and security demanded constant action.

He spoke for a program to consolidate the power and prestige of the union:

"The United Steelworkers of America must not for many months longer be known as the second largest union. It must be known as the largest union in America. And it's up to you to do it. I am not for size alone, because size alone means nothing. I ask it because of what it means to the people of America."

He noted that the charter issued originally by the CIO to the Steelworkers is "awfully broad" and stressed, "I'm not talking about raiding—I'm talking about organizing the unorganized."

As a starter, he announced a new drive of metal miners in the West, most of whom then were represented by the Mine, Mill, and Smelter Workers—a union booted out of the CIO because of Communist domination.

He outlined studies looking to the possibility of organizing iron ore miners in new ore fields of Latin-America and in bauxite mines of Jamaica.

113

He charted other union goals: a guaranteed annual wage to "wipe out fear of depression and poverty"; improved pensions; better social insurance protection; more liberal workmen's compensation and unemployment insurance.

Of the past record and future goals of the USA, McDonald declared:

"I am so proud of the Steelworkers' union and the things it has done in 16 short years that sometimes I almost explode.

"We have set some new goals and I think we are going to reach them because we have never yet failed in anything we started out to do. I think we have just scratched the surface in our endeavor to create a fuller and happier life for men and women of the United Steelworkers and all the people of America.

"Our creed will be to ever look and build for the future. With the cooperation and loyalty of our people and the help of Almighty God we cannot fail."

Later, at a joint national conference of the Blue Cross and Blue Shield in Hollywood, Florida, April 13, 1953, he elaborated on the goal of better social insurance, warning:

"Unless adequate medical and hospital care is provided by private means, the American people may demand compulsory Federal health insurance."

Three aims of his union to improve social insurance clauses in its wage agreements, he said, were: early diagnostic and preventive medical care; payment of medical, dental, drug and appliance bills; payment of all hospital bills.

"If your organizations rise to the challenge," McDonald told Blue Cross—Blue Shield officials, "we are willing to go forward with you."

On government affairs, he had these views:

"I think I am correct when I say that we can expect nothing in the way of advances from the new Administration and Congress in Washington. It may be that we will have to fight might and main to keep them from taking things away from us.

"But we will live under the Republican Administration (of Eisenhower) and we will grow under the Republican Administration, though it will be a new experience for us.

"With the aid of some friends, I've opened some doors in Washington. And they are not just tiny cracks. They are wide-open doors. If need be, we, the United Steelworkers, can enter through these doors. But I feel we cannot expect the type of help we got from our dear friend, Harry S. Truman.

"Beware of the Communists," he warned in a closing swipe at his favorite target, "they don't like us."

"The orders have gone out to do a job on the United Steelworkers. They are going to get active with their slimy borings from within; these things that crawl in the night are trying to bore from within some of our local unions. Thwart them wherever they rear their ugly heads!"

His advancement to the Presidency meant a nice pay

115

boost to $40,000 a year. The salary had been upped from $25,000 the previous year.

However, this was only slight balm for missing out on the big CIO prize. While Murray held the twin jobs of President of the Steelworkers and parent CIO, the latter plum had been plucked off by Walter Reuther, head of the United Auto Workers.

The "old guard" forces of Murray-McDonald, supporting colorful Allan Haywood, found themselves defeated by Reuther's "young Turks" in the CIO election at Atlantic City in December 1952.

It was a bitter disappointment for the Steelworkers to be displaced by Reuther. As the back-bone of the CIO, they considered the Presidency to be theirs historically— at least to the point of having a say about who got the job.

Haywood, a tired and broken man, died a few weeks later.

His No. 2 job of executive Vice-President and organizing director of the CIO went to John Riffe, a steelworker. Newspapers viewed this as a concession by Reuther to the Steelworkers.

At the UAW convention in Atlantic City in March of 1953, McDonald poured oil on the troubled waters. He told a story about a little girl, who had gotten into a bad habit of using profane words she heard her father say around the house.

"So, one day," he related, "this little girl, a tot about five years of age, was invited to a party.

"Her mother warned, 'all right, Mary, you can go to the party provided you don't use any of that nasty language. You must remember you are not allowed to swear when you go to that party.'

"The little girl said: 'All right, Mommie, I promise!'

"She got dressed up in her best dress and she went to the party. About half an hour later, she came home crying as though her heart were broken.

"Her mother said 'Uh-huh, you have been using foul language, you have disgraced us in the neighborhood. Okay, young lady, right up to your room and take off your good dress. And you stay up there until your father comes home, and he will take care of you for this.'

"At 5:30, in the evening, the old man came home. His wife said to him, 'Now, you have done it, you have been using this foul language, and now, Mary has disgraced us in the whole neighborhood. You go on upstairs to her room and handle this situation. I can't do a thing about it.'

"So, the old man went up and told Mary, 'Young lady, what have you been doing? You have been using foul language again. Is that why you got chased home from the party?'

" 'No, Daddy, the damn party was yesterday.' "

"That is the way I feel about this December situation," McDonald told the United Auto Workers, "that damn party was yesterday."

Hitting at the rumors of secession, he went on to explain that the United Steelworkers had too big an investment in

117

the CIO to ever think of pulling out of the organization, as rumored.

In a dramatic plea for unity, he ticked off figures that added up to a USA investment of $15,672,539.59 in the CIO.

"And that ain't hay," he noted.

The breakdown included $8,051,431.68 in dues; $1,621,-344 in the CIO Southern organizing campaign; $2,184,000 in salaries and expenses for personnel assigned to the CIO; $2,125,525 for cash contributions or cancelled loans to affiliates; and $1,690,431.91 to the CIO Political Action Committee, not counting treasury contributions to state candidates.

"Now, I ask you, in view of this," he told 3000 cheering delegates, "would we idly cast away such an investment? Why, of course not! We would no sooner cast away an investment like that than the General Motors Corporation would cast away the investment in the Cadillac plants. This has been an investment for the good of the people of America, and we, the United Steelworkers, are extremely proud that God has been so good to us that we have been able to invest this money."

Going on to admit that he had been meeting with representatives of the American Federation of Labor, as reported, Dave denied rumors that the USA planned to bolt the CIO, explaining:

"It is our intention to lead from strength unitedly and not from weakness divided . . . yes, we desire organic unity on a thoroughly, completely honorable basis, and on that basis alone."

Then, he launched into a story about frustration, revolving around two fellows who were sitting in a lonely, little bar in Pittsburgh at 3 o'clock in the morning discussing the difference between irritation, aggravation, and frustration. The one character finally said:

" 'Look, I can't explain it, but I can demonstrate it.' And he walked over to the telephone and said, 'I will show you irritation.'

"He dialed a number, picked at random, and a sleepy voice answered, 'Hello.'

"He asked, 'Is Mr. Winterbottom there?'

"The reply was, 'There is no Mr. Winterbottom here.' What number are you calling?'

"Grant 1-1235"

"The sleepy fellow said, 'There ain't any Winterbottom here,' and hung up.

"Twenty minutes later, the same character went to the telephone and said, 'I will now show you aggravation,' and he dialed the same number again. The same voice responded.

"He said, 'Is Mr. Winterbottom there?'

"The reply was, 'I told you no, Mr. Winterbottom is not here. What is the idea of calling me up at twenty minutes after three in the morning? Don't you have any more sense than that?'

"Bang went the phone. But twenty minutes later, the

119

same character explained. 'Now, I will show you what frustration means!' He dialed the same number and the same voice answered.

"The fellow at the bar said, 'This is Mr. Winterbottom. Have you had any calls for me?'

"Well," McDonald concluded, "I don't know as it fits in any place, but it is the sort of story I kind of like."

He added that "we are not going to be frustrated in any of these endeavors of ours, not at all . . . we are going to push on unitedly to achieve our goals."

With a bow in the direction of Reuther, the Man of Steel declared, "we will go onward, forward, building a greater, stronger, happier, more successful Congress of Industrial Organization, working side by side. God Bless You."

However, three months later, in June of 1953, there was speculation the reported breach between the Steelworkers and Reuther had reached the point that the USA might pull out of the CIO and form a third labor federation with the miners.

This was touched off by a meeting between McDonald and John L. Lewis, president of the United Mine Workers, in Washington. The meeting came after they had conferred by telephone for more than a month. They had been closely associated since McDonald started his labor career with the miners and Lewis was the leading force in organizing the steel union when he was head of the CIO. Coal and steel also are closely related basic industries. So, they had much in common.

"It is no secret," the *Pittsburgh Press* reported, "that Mr. McDonald and Mr. Reuther do not see eye to eye on how the CIO should be operated. There also have been reports that the head of the CIO Auto Workers (Reuther) was favoring his own organization at the financial expense of the Steelworkers.

"If the Steelworkers pulled their more than 1,000,000 members out of the CIO, it was considered likely that the CIO would break up as a major power in the labor field. Such a walkout probably would find the leaders of other CIO affiliates leading their flocks either to the new coal-steel combine or to the A.F. of L. unions."

The rumored steel-coal merger was not denied until six weeks after the Washington conference. McDonald finally claimed he was "only renewing old acquaintances" with Lewis. The delay in denying the rumor apparently was aimed at hastening CIO-AFL amalgamation, as McDonald was a member of a CIO subcommittee attempting to negotiate a merger with the A.F. of L.

Meanwhile, Reuther's moves to get fixed annual productivity and escalator clauses, tied to the cost of living, for the auto workers, drew an open challenge from McDonald.

"The Lord help labor," Dave was quoted, "if it ever gets tied to the cost of living."

To back up this point, he told the story of an old mineworker in Pennsylvania who objected to what he thought was a sliding-scale clause in a coal contract.

121

"What zips up," the old miner muttered, "must zip down."

McDonald also protested the plan of the CIO to eliminate its regional office in Pittsburgh. This was part of a proposal to reduce regional CIO offices from 36 to 13.

It was pointed out that Pittsburgh, center of Steel, without a CIO office would be like "ham without eggs." Plans to close the office were stymied.

After Reuther took over the CIO Presidency, the Steelworkers made another significant move in shifting their Washington offices in the crowded CIO building near the White House to a big, new air-conditioned building.

Decorated in beige and brown, with modernistic furniture, similar to the main offices in Pittsburgh's Commonwealth Building, the new Washington suites compared favorably with the U.S. Steel Corporation's offices a block away. This was in line with the growing stature of labor.

Through the 1940s, the years had been full of heartache such as only a lonely man can know. Finally this harried and intensely busy man found happiness when he married again in 1950. His bride was the former Rosemary McHugh, a charming brunet from Hazelton, Pennsylvania, who had been his Washington secretary.

The 1940s also had been full of frustration that any ambitious man feels when he is in the same job for a long time. Those who followed his career will tell you that McDonald remained loyally in the background. His role was something of the master mason of the pedestal that lifted the richly-gifted elder labor statesman, Murray, into the high public position that he won and held.

Dave declines even to discuss his own role during the remarkable Steelworker Era of 1936–52, saying only:

"That's the Phil Murray story. He was the boss and the hero. I just worked for him." Nevertheless, the McDonald story is the saga of the quality and dimensions of that work.

On reaching the Presidency, McDonald found that even bigger hurdles lay ahead. He found his very willingness and physical capacity increased the calls for his talents.

Being responsible for the economic welfare of more than a million steelworker families provided the greatest challenge of all. He also learned that his new position had its deep satisfactions as well as its demands. One occasion that should have given him a deep draft of pride and satisfaction, also wrote a new chapter in labor-management history.

Ardent union supporters decided to mark his first year in the president's chair with a city-wide celebration in his home town of Pittsburgh. That was on Saturday, the twenty-eighth of November, 1953.

Mayor David L. Lawrence officially proclaimed DAVID J. McDONALD DAY. Shortly thereafter, the affair took on an international aspect when the labor attaches of the United Kingdom, France, Germany and Canada joined in the preparations.

Two weeks prior to the dinner, Dave and Benjamin F. Fairless, Chairman of the Board of United States Steel, had begun a series of plant tours, meeting the men in the mills.

This must have been headline news even to departed labor leaders in the great beyond.

Then, Fairless accepted the committee's invitation to be one of the principal speakers at a testimonial which had now become a labor-management get-together.

Mayor-Elect Robert F. Wagner, Jr., both a warm friend of McDonald and a good friend of labor, was invited by a committee that called on him at his campaign headquarters in the Biltmore Hotel on November 2nd.

Perhaps the most zestful note of this most unusual occasion was the huge sendoff it rated on page one of the *Wall Street Journal,* surely a strange place to find a happy account of the doings of organized labor. But there it was:

PITTSBURGH BANNERED, LIGHTED AND BEDECKED, STAGING "DAY FOR DAVE"

*   *   *

DINNERS, TELEVISED SPEECHES, FLOOR SHOWS TO HONOR STEEL-WORKERS' CHIEF McDONALD

By Edward J. Lally

Staff Reporter of The Wall Street Journal

PITTSBURGH—More than 3,000 men and women from labor and industry, religion and education, politics and the professions will turn out here tomorrow night to honor David J. McDonald as Pittsburgh's "man of steel."

It will be quite an affair.

Streets, railroad stations, hotel lobbies and the airport will be decorated for the occasion, an elaborate testimonial for the 51-year-old leader of the C.I.O. United Steelworkers.

If plans of the committee in charge are fulfilled, all downtown Pittsburgh buildings will be lighted from top to bottom and honored guests will be taken to the top of a hill overlooking the city to see the sight.

The mayor-elect of New York City and the chairman of United States Steel Corp. will speak at the main testimonial banquet in the William Penn Hotel. Their words will be piped to a satellite dinner in the Roosevelt Hotel several blocks away.

"DAY FOR DAVE"

General chairman of "David J. McDonald Day" is William J. Hart, director of United Steelworkers' District 19, covering the north side and Lawrenceville sections of Pittsburgh and the Allegheny River Valley northeast of here.

Mr. Hart, a dynamic labor personality who also serves on Pittsburgh's Board of Public Education, is generally credited with inspiring the special "Day for Dave." He has termed the testimonial the "most important labor-management undertaking ever planned"

125

and a "great tribute celebrating labor's role in the New Pittsburgh."

His committee has left little undone to make the affair live up to the rave notices he himself posted for it.

Steelworkers from as far away as California will rub shoulders with hundreds of management people, including some of the shiniest brass in the steel industry. Labor attaches representing the United Kingdom, Canada, France and West Germany will be on hand.

BANNERS AT THE AIRPORT

Visitors arriving by plane will see McDonald banners and bunting strung up in the modernistic administration building of the new Greater Pittsburgh Airport. For those coming by train, there will be pictures of Mr. McDonald in the railroad stations, and for home towners there will be street decorations in the "Golden Triangle" business district.

Hotel lobbies will display pictures of the steel union's leader, a Pittsburgh native who started out in the mills as a machinist's helper for 22 cents an hour and who became steelworkers' president about a year ago following the death of Philip Murray.

Those who go to the William Penn Hotel for the main festivities will pay $20 a plate. Some steel companies have taken tables for 10 at $200 a table. Guests at the Roosevelt Hotel will get by for $15 a plate and while they won't be at the chief attraction, they will, during the evening, be visited by Mr. McDonald, the guest of honor, Mayor-Elect Robert F. Wagner, Jr. of New York, and Benjamin F. Fairless, U. S. Steel chairman, the chief speakers.

The ticket price also covers a floor show and musical programs to be presented between 6:30 and 8 o'clock. Speeches by Mr. Fairless, Mr. Wagner and others will be broadcast and the entire evening's program will be filmed for television.

———

That is not all of the story, but surely enough to make it plain that *The Journal,* at least on this occasion, had taken a new look at Labor.

In a very real sense, the celebration of David J. Mc-Donald Day gave the entire City of Pittsburgh an opportunity to take a "new look" at labor. Pittsburgh itself, having begun a gigantic re-development program in 1945, had good reason to assay the contribution made by labor— as well as Labor's continuing role—in the *new* Pittsburgh, as it was generally recognized.

Bishop Austin Pardue of the Episcopal Diocese of Pittsburgh epitomized this new recognition when he spoke of McDonald's place in the city and the nation:

"Dave McDonald has grown in the inner life and has thus achieved at a youthful age one of the highest posts to be occupied in our great free land.

"May God grant that he continue to grow in these eternal characteristics and thereby attain the exalted destiny that the Creator of mankind has, in His infinite wisdom, ordained to be accomplished."

President Eisenhower sent Maxwell Rabb as his personal representative and wired his greetings to Dave. There were wires from Harry Truman and Adlai Stevenson, as well.

Amid all the fanfare, some of the oldtimers could remember the time when—in all of Pittsburgh and Allegheny County—there was no place for a union meeting. Small wonder they came from as far away as the West Coast and from 70 cities and towns.

The new guard and the old guard could look to the long speakers' table and see there a young man whose father had secured passage of organized labor's "Magna Carta"—the Wagner Labor Relations Act.

Robert F. Wagner, Jr., son of the late Senator from New York State, was now the Mayor-Elect of the nation's largest city.

Said Bob Wagner:

"The very proof that labor achieved a partnership with industry that it had never had before is in this room, with the presence of Mr. Fairless on the dais. There are some who can remember the days when a corporation executive would not have spoken at a union dinner, in fact he wouldn't have spoken to a union member. And as far as eating at a union dinner is concerned, he would have preferred to eat the union, or otherwise dispose of it.

"But those days are gone. Now, Mr. Fairless and Mr. McDonald are touring the steel plants together, discussing conditions, talking to the men and the plant superintendents, doing everything they can to see that the United

128

States Steel Company and the United Steelworkers of America are partners in the task of building a greater and stronger and more prosperous America. If they succeed, they will also be building a greater, and more peaceful world, and for that they will have earned the thanks of every responsible citizen and every responsible nation."

How to hold fast to today's gains and include the public in the industry-management partnership was clearly defined by Mr. Fairless—and he was roundly cheered by the thousands of steel workers who heard him and met him in two hotels.

Aptly, Mr. Fairless chose to speak on "The Task Ahead."

"Americans are a patient people," he said, "but they will not go on forever allowing us to settle our private quarrels at the expense of the public welfare."

Stating his recognition and support of labor's right to organize and bargain collectively, the Chairman of the Board of United States Steel said labor and management *must:*

1. Improve collective bargaining methods.

2. Eliminate the "endless and senseless succession of strikes."

"I know that both of us want to find that better way," said Mr. Fairless, "but we shall never do so in an atmosphere of recrimination, suspicion and distrust of each other's motives. We can only do so in an atmosphere of mutual respect, understanding and confidence in one another.

129

"To create that respect, understanding and confidence, of course, will take infinite patience, endless perseverance, and a great willingness on both sides to understand the other fellow's problems and his point of view. But among men of intelligence, reason, and good will it is by no means an impossible task."

Looking about the great room or any of the rooms which were packed with guests, it was easy to see that Ben Fairless was talking the kind of language they had always hoped to hear from management. The industry men in the audience were plainly proud of management's position so well stated.

"Actually, of course, our interests are identical," said Fairless. "For better or worse, we are inseparably bound together in a state of economic matrimony. We live in the same industrial household, and the individual welfare of each of us depends entirely on the strength and security of the household itself."

Many who attended that "Dinner for Dave" found a double satisfaction in the event.

Reasonably enough, they felt they had been "there" when history was made in the Steel Capital of the World.

CHAPTER 10

THE SEVENTH ROUND

On TAKING OVER the Presidency of the United Steelworkers, Dave McDonald immediately installed an "open door" policy.

Members of the union's International Wage Policy Committee—composed of "140 guys from the mills, mines and factories, plus the 30-man executive board"—were asked to siphon up the ideas from the rank and file.

"Under this system," Dave explained, "they have a chance to express themselves and I have a chance to listen. In this way, we not only get a good cross-section of opinion, but some swell ideas that we wouldn't get otherwise."

That's how the McDonald administration came up with the wage agreement in May 1953—and cleared its first big hurdle.

Negotiating for a new contract—hardly before he had a chance to warm up his chair—provided the toughest kind of baptismal fire for the new President.

The cards were stacked against him. Along with the 61-day strike of the previous year, the Steelworkers had set the pace for six nationwide wage increases since the war. They were in an uncomfortable bargaining spot to make it seven.

On the other side of the table, the steel industry sat in its best bargaining position in years. It could point to many reasons, economic and otherwise, why the workers should not get a raise.

Through its newspaper *Steel Labor,* the union launched an early campaign to take the edge off anti-strike sentiment. A front-page story, headlining "The 1952 Strike—It Paid Dividends," argued that lost wages of $597.44 a member had been more than offset by the 12½ cent an hour increase.

Less vacation pay of $149.00 and $83.20 won as retroactive pay, the average maximum temporary loss was figured at $264.88. Against this, the article pointed out, the average weekly pay increase under the contract that ended the strike amounted to $10.88.

On this basis, increased pay from the end of the strike to March 31, 1953, totalled $380.80—or slightly more than the pay lost during the idleness.

Every year in the future, *Steel Labor* claimed, steelworkers will earn $565.76 more than they did before the strike.

Prior to negotiations, John Delaney, writing in the steel

industry magazine *Iron Age,* on May 14, 1953, sketched
this picture of McDonald:

"He resents speculation that he will be a 'pushover' in
his first dealings with the steel industry. . . . In some re-
spects, he is more conservative (than Murray) in reflecting
the thinking of his membership. He is inclined to lean
more heavily on others in the union hierarchy in mapping
out his program. He may not have the flair and 'color' of
Murray, but he is potentially as capable in achieving union
aims.

"There is no reason to believe that McDonald will be
any easier to deal with than Philip Murray."

Later that month, Dave took the spotlight on the labor
stage for the first time. He led a delegation of union com-
mitteemen into a conference room in Pittsburgh to negotiate with U. S. Steel officials. He sat in the chairman's seat,
the first time in 17 years that it had been held by anyone
but Murray.

However, Dave was no newcomer at the bargaining
table. Through the years, he had been at Murray's side,
serving with Clinton S. Golden and Van A. Bittner, Pres-
idential Assistants, as one of the "Big Four" negotiators
for the steelworkers. He had a knack for this sort of thing.

Once during a tense negotiating session, when tempers
were near the breaking point, Dave had turned on a radio
broadcast of a World Series baseball game. The others
joined him. When the last out was called, negotiations re-
sumed in a much calmer atmosphere.

In announcing that the Steelworkers' union was reopening its contract to seek a general wage boost, McDonald bluntly told the industry representatives:

"The men in the mills are tired of eating margarine . . . they want butter."

Main goal of his union, he said, was improvement of living standards of its members—"more money to make payments on autos . . . to buy electric refrigerators . . . to get better homes."

It was a tough argument to sell. The base wage in steel had increased from 78 cents during the war to an average rate of $2.06 an hour. In six rounds, the hourly rate climbed 9¼ cents in January, 1946; 9¼ cents in February, 1947; 12½ cents in April, 1947; then 9½ cents in July, 1948; and two raises of 12½ cents each in December, 1950 and March, 1952.

This added a total of 65½ cents to the base level of $1.43½ for the minimum job, class-one level. American Iron and Steel Institute compiled figures indicating that— with fringe benefits for insurance, pensions, paid vacation, holidays, shift differentials and overtime, the labor cost to the steel industry averaged $2.38 an hour.

But this still wasn't enough to provide the things that McDonald wanted for the steelworkers.

The new chairman of the union negotiating committee sailed through his first big test in a fashion that raised the eyebrows of oldtimers. He secured a seventh-round wage increase totalling about ten cents an hour—without strike or threat of strike.

Even John A. Stephens, veteran bargainer for U. S. Steel, paid McDonald the rare compliment of saying he had done a "good statesmanlike job."

And Big Steel, once again, had set the national pace. Other industries followed the steel pattern.

During the Summer of 1953, the union's research department reported that both hourly and weekly earnings reached all-time highs. Hourly earnings averaged $2.21 and weekly earnings $91.05 in July. Since 1936, hourly wages increased from 66 cents an hour, rising 236 per cent while the cost of living went up less than 100 per cent. On top of this were pensions, social insurance, paid vacations, and holiday benefits.

Steel production, running at an estimated 95 per cent of capacity, also was expected to reach an all-time high in 1953 of some seven million tons over the all-time record year of 1951.

In its first year, the McDonald administration also chalked up a new high in membership. Organizing, a long suit of the new president, boosted the total to 1,180,000 men and women employed in 2300 steel mills, fabricating shops, aluminum mills, ore mines, and factories throughout the United States and Canada.

There is no way of determining with any certainty whether this makes the United Steelworkers the largest union or not. Dues, paid to the CIO on the basis of 10 cents per member per month, are the measuring stick. The Steelworkers, with books completely audited by an outside accounting firm, pay on actual memberships. Some other unions, not employing outside auditors, could claim larger memberships simply by paying heavier monthly dues to the parent group than actual membership.

"We pay on what we get," is McDonald's terse comment.

In any event, the USA rates as one of the "Big Three" with the A. F. of L. Teamsters and CIO United Auto Workers.

The USA in 1953 gained many new members in the "white collar" field.

By late summer, nearly 40,000 held USA cards. Since the first contract in 1941 with National Tube Company— McDonald's "Alma Mater," where he worked in the store-room and machine shop of the Hazelwood works as a 15-year-old boy, the salary of "white collar" workers increased more than $200 a month. Fringe benefits, on top of that, included: a $100 minimum monthly pension for 25 years service at age 65; social security for employes and dependents; paid vacations; overtime pay; extra pay plus time off for holidays worked; premium pay for afternoon and night shifts.

The average monthly salary of messengers, for example, jumped from $58.00 to $241.00, up more than four times. Substantial gains also were passed along to clerical employes, including supervisory personnel and others not eligible for union membership.

More than 120 companies had signed "white collar" agreements with the USA. Many others dealt with office locals through special sections written into production and maintenance agreements.

"No longer is the risk of unfair discharge one of the prices to be paid for wearing a white collar to work," McDonald declared in August of 1953.

"However, we've got to do more with this group," he added later, with the view that it will play an increasingly important role in the steel industry.

On the delicate subject of union-management relations, President McDonald wasted no time putting himself on record as always standing ready to co-operate.

In a speech, shortly after taking office, he declared:

"We co-operate with management when co-operation is offered to us in the interests of protecting and improving the conditions of our members. We always seek such co-operation but we know we must be ready at all times for sharp struggles against management when the conditions of our members are endangered or retarded by short-sighted management policies.

"We believe that sincere co-operation between labor and industry is most desirable. It will serve everyone's best interests. We work for government policies which encourage such co-operation.

"American labor is constantly working for the welfare of the whole nation. When the union worker gets a pay boost, this encourages improved methods of production

137

and expansion of industry. Higher wages also enable workers to buy the farmers' products and use services of the
professional people. Thus, prosperity for the worker has a
chain-reaction on other groups."

Along with industrial prosperity, he pledged to actively
strive for improvements in education, medical service,
housing, recreational programs and every phase of American life.

Pointing out that labor's security and progress is tied
in with the welfare of people everywhere, the Man of Steel
explained:

"That's why we support democratic movements and
progressive policies throughout the world just as we oppose Communism and every other force working to re-
strict or destroy freedom and human welfare."

"While the American system has been good to labor,"
he warned, "we have no illusions about it providing
some magic way to help people."

"We do not seek an easy way," McDonald concluded.

"There is none.

"We have the right to work for our own ideas and
interests. What we have we have won through great effort
and sacrifice. We are prepared to make any sacrifice to
keep what we have.

"What we have includes the right to go forward to
new achievements. Through the American system of private capitalism and industrial democracy, we know we will
make ever greater progress."

While a staunch defender of labor's rights, the Man of Steel has very strong ideas about the sacredness of a contract—and the obligation on both sides to live up to it.

"There are two phases of industrial relations," he explains. "Only one of them usually comes to public attention. That is when an agreement is being negotiated, sometimes marked by a strike.

"The other part is the day-by-day housekeeping of industrial relations, after an agreement has been reached. That is the real stabilizing element in labor-management relations.

"Once a contract has been signed, both sides should do their level, honest best to live up to that agreement. A contract is a sacred obligation to be observed by both parties. It is the basis of sound industrial relations. Through the use of grievance and arbitration machinery, as spelled out in the contract, we really have democracy in action."

This point was emphasized in no uncertain fashion during a wildcat strike in Bethlehem Steel Company's Lackawanna mills during September 1953.

In a telegram to Joseph Larkin, industrial relations vice-president for Bethlehem Steel, McDonald put himself flatly in the position of living up to the "no strike" clause in the contract.

Pointing out that an orderly procedure for settling grievances had been set up in the contract, he reassured Larkin that:

"The United Steelworkers of America is a responsible union. It is proud of its contracts and it regards these contracts both as a legal and moral obligation to be faithfully performed on its part and on the part of the company in good faith."

Both the union and the companies should "scrupulously adhere" to their contracts, the wire concluded.

It left no doubt in the minds of officials in the field and in local unions just where President McDonald stood.

This policy also served as a stabilizing force in relations between the union and industry.

A champion and active participant in political action since formation of the CIO's Political Action Committee in 1943, McDonald believes labor must take an active part and interest both in state and federal legislation.

If laws can't be passed in the National Congress, then he says they should be tackled in State Legislatures to improve conditions in such fields as health and safety, unemployment and workmen's compensation and fair employment practices.

"In many cases," he explains, "legislation may indirectly be just as important a 'bread and butter' issue to steelworkers as a wage increase or a grievance settlement."

Unemployment compensation, workmen's compensation, and many other fields such as taxation were cited as examples of this.

His political views were detailed in an educational pamphlet used at Summer Institutes in 1953:

"We believe that the union must represent the viewpoint of the worker in speaking up, for or against, legislative action that would help or harm him . . .

"For instance, when a man is injured and unable to work, or when he is unemployed through no fault of his own, he needs help of an extraordinary nature. The United Steelworkers of America wants to be in a position to help him. . . .

"The primary mission in life for any sincere trade union is to promote the welfare of its members and to strive for an ever-improving standard of living for their families. The main avenue of approach in fulfilling that mission, of course, is to be found in the realm of collective bargaining. . . .

"Through collective bargaining, wage agreements are written, grievances settled and countless problems resolved in the day-to-day relationship of management and union committees.

"The United Steelworkers of America, however, has never been content to stop at that point. We believe we can be of tremendous help to the steelworkers and their families in many other important ways.

"We believe, for instance, that the gains won through collective bargaining must be protected as much as possible against legislative attacks which would nullify them.

"In other words, we believe that our union can lend a degree of protection to steelworkers when they are con-

141

fronted by a situation which cannot be resolved through ordinary collective bargaining."

In charting a political course, McDonald thinks that unions must be flexible, explaining:

"We support policies of the government when they are good for the people. We oppose them when they are bad for the people."

He claims that unions are "politically independent because we owe allegiance only to our members, not to any political group or political leaders."

Appearing before the House Committee on Education and Labor to testify on the Taft-Hartley Law, McDonald objected to the emergency provisions of the act which calls for the use of injunctions in walkouts threatening the welfare of the nation, as well as a vote by employes on the final management offer.

"This provision," he said at the hearing in April of 1953, "apparently assumes that the management of a corporation truly speaks for the owners—the stockholders—while the representatives of a union cannot really speak for its owners—the members.

"His (management's) spokesmanship . . . is unquestioned under the act. Ours is, despite the fact that we are much more responsive to the views of our 'owners' than the average management representative."

Dave also objected to the provisions of Taft-Hartley which required the union to file non-Communist affidavits with the National Labor Relations Board and financial reports with the U. S. Department of Labor.

The Steelworkers' constitution bars Communists from any position of leadership at any level in the union and financial statements, including semi-annual audits, always have been made public, he pointed out.

Sections of the act which set up rules to govern relations between craft and industrial unions also were criticized. Neither the union nor the employers have any assurance under this provision that they will not have to go through jurisdictional elections year after year, he explained.

The Man of Steel told the House Committee that the union is "vitally interested in avoiding or settling nationwide walkouts among the steel companies. There have been three such strikes (1946, 1949, and 1952) since the union was formed in 1936.

"In each case," he said, "we postponed our strikes when so requested by the government."

"In each case, we accepted government proposals for settlement of the dispute, despite the extent to which these proposals denied what we considered reasonable requests for improvements in working conditions.

"Our union does not lightly engage in strikes. We are aware of the consequences to all concerned, to our nation, to our members and their families, and to the employers. A cessation of operations affects our members more in-

143

timately and deeply than it does either the employer or the stockholders."

At the same time, McDonald wanted to correct an impression that the union was "coercing" the steel companies of the nation into national settlements based on patterns established in negotiations with the big firms.

"How can a union, worth ten million, 'coerce' an industry with a net worth of six billion dollars?" he wanted to know.

"It is apparent, from these figures," he told the committee, "that this union, although healthy, is in no economic position to coerce the industry."

Observers noted that the union president overlooked the point that the economic burden of a strike is borne by members of the union, not the treasury of the international. Figured on a net worth of $1000 per member, the resources the union can use in an economic struggle would go well over the billion dollar mark, it was pointed out.

It was in this same political arena that the Man of Steel made several of his rare "slips." Although usually careful about what he says on any subject, his ability to turn a phrase and flip it off on the spur of the moment got him into hot water at a Political Action Committee organizing meeting in Harrisburg, Pennsylvania, in 1944.

As finance chairman of the National PAC, McDonald told 300 CIO representatives:

"I hope we get twenty-five million dollars. We want all

144

we can get. The more we get, the more we can spend. The more we spend, the better Congress we will have. The more we spend in Pennsylvania, the better state legislature we will have. It's as simple as that."

This startling statement was interpreted in various newspapers as meaning that the way to win elections is to buy them. They put him in the bag with the Mark Hannas, Boss Tweeds, Boise Penroses and other famous advocates of the boodle-bag in elections.

Coming at a time when men were dying on the battlefield, it stirred up quite a rumpus. The statement quickly was discounted by Sidney Hillman, national president of the CIO Political Action Committee, who declared that McDonald was not authorized to speak for the national group.

On another occasion, early in 1952, just before President Harry S. Truman seized the steel industry, USA Secretary-Treasurer McDonald made another speech declaring that the Steelworkers' union had nothing to worry about because there was a "rather friendly gentleman in the White House."

This touched off wide speculation that an advance committment had been made to the Steelworkers that Truman wouldn't use the Taft-Hartley Act.

What he actually meant, Dave explained, was that the man in the White House realized that the working man had basic rights in the field of pay, benefits and working conditions.

145

Later that year, in June of 1952, the "friendly gentleman" statement was offset somewhat by a sly dig at the Truman administration.

The details were related by McDonald, with tongue in cheek, in a letter to Anthony J. Federoff, chairman of the CIO Government and Civic Employes Organizing Committee. The letter was carried in the organizing committee's publication *Service*.

Dave told of finding a description of the government's incentive-award system at the Federal Security Agency in Washington. Under the system, employees with 10, 20 and 30 years service rated a bronze emblem and certificate bearing a FACSIMILE of the administrator's signature. Those with 40 years' service, however, rated a gold emblem and certificate with the administrator's ACTUAL signature.

"Thus," McDonald concluded in his letter to Federoff, "I have finally discovered the basic reason why it is so difficult to organize employes of the federal government."

CHAPTER 11

AMERICAN CAPITALISM AND COMMUNISM

MOST LABOR LEADERS shy away from all-out endorsement of the American capitalistic system.

Not Dave McDonald. The international President of the CIO United Steelworkers accepts "democratic capitalism" without reservation because he believes American workers profit when the system profits.

He has pledged himself to stand side by side with industry in fighting depression.

He knows that high wages and production remove poverty; that steady smoke from the open hearth stacks means new cars for the workers.

He believes that science, industry and labor form a "Big Three" that can lick hunger, disease and want in peaceful times as well as in war.

Staunch defender of American free enterprise, the Man

of Steel outlined his views in a State Department broadcast beamed to Western Europe early in 1953:

"The American system is private capitalism bolstered by industrial democracy and served by a vigorous, free government. There is no rigid blueprint that can describe the American system.

"It differs from one part of the country to the next, from one industry to the next, from one decade to the next.

"It is a system of change, growth and continuing progress.

"In the process of change, growth and progress, the workers of our country exert a great influence on all phases of American life.

"One of the most important tasks of labor is performed at the industry and plant level. The thousands of decisions made by foremen, superintendents, directors and industry-wide employers' associations necessarily must give weight to the desires of workers as expressed by their unions.

"The great growth of unions during the past 20 years has made industrial democracy a vital part of American life. The democracy enjoyed by the worker is not fully revealed by the big events in collective bargaining about which so much is heard and read.

"The daily local influences over job rights, promotional opportunities, work loads, opportunities for mealtime and rest periods, safety methods, and innumerable other matters important to the worker

148

add up to a most significant part of the growing democracy in American industry.

"In America, there is no single or dictated way by which the worker participates in determining wages and working conditions. Methods are developed which suit each particular situation.

"It is this right to do the job the way that works best which is a source of great strength to the American system.

"American labor likes it this way. We find that the American system enables workers to organize, unite and co-operate most effectively and without continual dictation either by the heads of industry or by the heads of government.

"Our job is never finished because we always seek greater prosperity for our members, greater security, a higher standard of living for the nation, a happier community life and more desirable conditions on the job.

"As each victory is achieved, we have new goals to strive toward."

Outspoken champion of democratic capitalism, the Man of Steel also has been a long-time foe of Communism, and its little brother, Socialism.

As he grew up with the labor movement, he had a front-line view of how the Reds operated during the slam-bang struggles of the 1920's.

Even before that, Dave had had an opportunity to assert his views when a blacksmith tried to convince him that Socialism was the answer to the workingman's problems.

No labor leader has a stronger or more consistent record of unwavering resistance to subversive influences.

As early as the strike of 1937, McDonald lashed out at the Reds. Serving then as secretary-treasurer of the Steelworkers Organizing Committee, he was the first CIO official to lay it on the line.

In a speech at Gary, Indiana, he denounced the Communists as enemies of labor. Declaring that the Reds were agents of the coal operators from 1925–28, he related experiences of their efforts to "bust" the miners' union.

Dave concluded that he "detested their philosophy and personally hated their leaders."

This was mighty strong language in those days. Vincent D. Sweeney, who left the *Pittsburgh Press* as a labor writer to direct public relations for the union, had a hot potato on his hands in deciding whether to run the story in *Steel Labor,* the official publication of the Steelworkers' union.

"I believe you're right," Vince finally told McDonald. "I'm going to do it. And I don't care what happens."

The speech was carried as the lead story in the union newspaper and made headlines from coast to coast.

It was policy-making in scope.

That same year, Dave had the "very great privilege of firing every Communist on the staff of the Steelworkers as quick as I could find them, despite bitter opposition of some colleagues. A lot of our friends were playing footsie with the Commies."

On March 1, 1940, he threw Fascism and Naziism into the same pot with the Commies, declaring that these "isms" never would have a voice in the union movement. Addressing the Massachusetts CIO convention at Worcester, Mass., he warned:

"There are people who would like to use the steelworkers' union to hold what they call 'classless society.' Agents of the Communist party, for instance, would like to turn the union into an instrument for their own use."

"However," he concluded, "neither the steelworkers nor the Steel Workers Organizing Committee intend to let this happen. Communism, Naziism and Fascism are equally iniquitous in their opposition to Democracy."

Later that same year at an Armistice Day flag dedication, part of the SWOC Americanization and Citizenship program, he told members of American Legion Post 531 in Pittsburgh:

"At a time when democracy has become almost a legend, it is up to the United States to demonstrate that it is a system which works well for the good of mankind. In addition to a great defense force, Americans must build an inner demonstration of democracy and solve the problems of unemployment and social maladjustment.

"Labor unions are essential in a democracy if that democracy is to function properly. There should be established in America economic councils for each major industry. These councils should consist of representatives of industry, labor and government. It should be their concern to solve satisfactorily the problems of each industry. Through a system of joint enterprise and co-operation of all these elements of our economic life a real unity of our people can be developed.

"Navies and armies cannot stop the borers from within once the enemies of democracy get into the minds of the people," he asserted.

Training his guns on Naziism, the steel union leader, in a radio speech on May 27, 1941, pointed out that only by destruction of the trade union movement in Germany had Adolf Hitler been able to bring Europe to its knees:

"Under the Hitler dictatorship, the whole of Central Europe was introduced to an economic system which indeed is worse than the system of human slavery of old times.

"We here in America must not fall into a trap in our efforts to thwart the advance of totalitarianism. We must not permit Hitler-minded politicians in Congress to throttle labor. These politicos use a vastly exaggerated strike situation as an excuse to destroy the fundamental rights of labor. They would like to remove the right of men to organize and to bargain collectively with their employer.

"This is a fundamental premise of our economy and because it is a fundamental premise, naturally it must be a fundamental premise of our democracy. Yet, these men in

America today are trying to destroy it, whether they realize it or not, they are trying to destroy our democracy."

After the war, when Russia turned from being a fighting ally and exposed its hand as the greatest threat of all to world peace, McDonald again went to work on the Communists.

In 1948, at a CIO-PAC rally in Canton, Ohio, he charged that the Communist Party had ordered its followers in the CIO United Steelworkers to "undermine the union."

The attack from within the Steelworkers, he said, had been ordered by the Communist high command as a result of the union's convention in Boston earlier that year. At the convention, the union overwhelmingly voted to bar Communists and other subversives or sympathizers from all union offices—local, district and international. This applied to committees and other delegations as well.

Part of the Red drive, he explained, was to tell union members not to sign the dues' check-off authorization cards that were being solicited under the Taft-Hartley Act. Failure to sign the cards meant loss of the employees' jobs in all plants where the company and Union had a contract calling for maintenance of membership or a union shop.

By the time McDonald advanced to the USA Presidency, the union had been pretty thoroughly cleared of Commies —at least in positions of leadership. And he could concentrate his attention on other matters.

Down through the years, when he wasn't crusading against the foreign "isms," Dave plugged hard for labor to play a more aggressive role in politics, for improvements in collective bargaining and for settling disagreements at the bargaining table instead of by strike.

At the Pennsylvania Institute of Certified Accountants convention in Bedford, Penna., June 16, 1941, he proposed that accountants should sit in at the conference table to help labor and management negotiate a new contract.

"Active participation of cost accounting experts in collective bargaining conferences," he explained, "would add much to the speedier resolving of the problems and at the same time eliminate much of the guess work and misstatements which developed.

"Furthermore, their presence would make it possible for the union representatives to obtain the honest exposition of cost factors from persons most familiar with the facts. Actual first-hand contact with workers and their union representatives would make the financial officers more conscious of the human equations involved.

"Their dry cost figures would become symbolic of flesh and blood, of men themselves, with families like theirs and problems of a similar nature."

At the same time, McDonald plumped for Murray's proposal to increase production of vital defense materials by establishing Industry Councils. Looking ahead, he saw the Councils helping to cushion the effect of a drop in production after the war. And he defended the demands for higher wages, by arguing that "high wages make nations prosperous and low wages make them failures."

In a bold maneuver few labor leaders would have risked taking, McDonald stepped into the 1946 strike of the independent union of the Duquesne Light Company.

With industrial Pittsburgh facing a blackout and paralysis, he appeared on a radio broadcast with the Rev. Charles Owen Rice, famed Pittsburgh labor priest, and condemned the strike, stating:

"Why should I, as an official of a CIO labor union, interest myself in the Duquesne Light Company industrial dispute? Simply, because I, as a citizen of this community, regret that the situation has developed to such a point that almost two million fellow citizens will be seriously discommoded, to say the least.

"Furthermore, because I believe that the impending strike need not occur, this much is absolutely certain; that if it does occur, it will have to be settled.

"Some day, somehow the strike will end. It should be ended before it begins. How? You ask. And the answer: by collective bargaining. It will end in that manner anyway, so why not do it now? That is, why not bargain collectively and in entire good faith?

"I know Pressly H. McCance (President of the Light Company). I served with him on various civic boards. I know that he engages in a form of bargaining during some

155

of the meetings of these boards. He is not the type of person whose mind is closed to reasoning.

"Perhaps he doesn't have the power to collectively bargain this issue between the company and the independent union of the Duquesne Light Company employees. If he has not the power, then he must obtain that power from those persons who do have the authority to give him the right to bargain.

"People can't sit in an ivory tower in some distant city and frustrate genuine collective bargaining in the City of Pittsburgh. Also, the day is here when no one is deceived by the type of propaganda concerning earnings which emanates from the office of the company. The boys in the ivory tower should have learned that lesson long ago. But evidently they have not.

"Do the employees of the Duquesne Light Company need an increase in wages? Of course they do. As I understand the situation, as of now, the company doesn't have a wage increase offer on the table. One proposal of a 7½ per cent increase was made, but it has since withdrawn that offer. A 7½ per cent offer isn't enough in my judgment.

"Many power companies, such as Consolidated Edison of New York, the Ohio Power Company, and others have negotiated agreements with the CIO, which represents their employees, for increases far in excess of the figure the Duquesne Light Company once proposed and which is now withdrawn . . . working people don't strike for the sheer fun of striking. There's no joy in striking. Believe me, I know. . . . They want a settlement. They need a raise in wages. No one in this day and age can dispute that fact.

"I don't pretend to understand all the economics involved in the immediate situation. But I understand that working people need increases today.

"The Mayor is trying to conciliate this. He is working hard. My advice to Mayor David L. Lawrence, not that he needs it, is to keep Pressly McCance and George Mueller (independent union president) together in collective bargaining sessions, continuously, until an accord is reached.

"Both sides must have complete authority to settle the dispute. Settle it now before the strike. Remember, it has to be settled some day anyway."

The strike still went on and Pittsburgh was paralyzed for 19½ hours until the dispute finally was submitted to arbitration.

Just as McDonald had predicted, it had to be settled at the bargaining table with federal arbiter, Aaron Horvitz, wangling a compromise settlement.

CHAPTER 12

THE NEW LOOK IN LABOR

ONTO THE mid-Twentieth Century scene has come a New Look in labor leaders.

Dave McDonald differs in many ways from the old-style unionist, both inside and out.

Bred in the union movement, he lived it to the hilt all of his life.

He experienced the struggle, pain, hardship and rewards.

He has fought just as hard as any of them for labor's gains.

Yet, the international President of the United Steelworkers has the ability to shake off the bitter past and to deal with things as they are.

Coming up through the mills and slugging it out with the college books in night courses, McDonald emerged like a piece of polished steel.

He could see both sides of the labor picture.

158

He could recognize that industrialists today are not the same as the hard-minded tycoons of the 1920's—that they have been replaced largely by practical, professional business executives.

He could see evidence on every side that today's business leaders recognize labor's changed position—that they insist only on not being pushed off the chair by labor, the government, or anyone else.

On his steadying performance in the basic steel industry rests much of the hope for peace in the labor-management field. To a considerable extent, the prosperity of the nation and the world, as well, is at stake.

One top industrialist, who has faced him across the arbitration table and admits getting none the better of it, sizes him up this way:

"Dave McDonald is the modern adaptation of Phil Murray. He takes a new approach in labor statesmanship with his ability to study all the angles, think things through and then reach a workable decision. He can give and take, but he is just as tough and shrewd as Murray ever was.

"You can discuss things and reason with McDonald. He will accept sincerity, but heaven help anyone who tries to slip one over on him. He can and does get bow-legged and just as nasty as any of the old-timers. On basic issues, though, he gets down to facts and cases.

"Dave McDonald is not a labor boss of the old school. He is a top-flight executive—practical and realistic. He knows that businessmen today are not horned monsters."

159

Getting right down to it, McDonald is a businessman himself. He has to be, to run things right. Because the Steelworkers union is big business with assets of close to $14,000,000 and yearly income of more than $40,000,000 in dues of $3.00 monthly.

Throughout the years, during his service as Secretary-Treasurer, never has any suspicion of dishonesty crept into the Steelworkers' union. A bargaining representative for management says:

"The steelworkers have been clean right from the start. No one in management would ever think of trying to grease them. You just wouldn't get anywhere. Yet, you hear on all sides about older unions and how some agents can be reached for concessions or favors."

While officials in other unions have been exposed or accused of having their fingers in the union insurance racket, the USA has consistently declined to have anything to do with insurance business. This was left in the hands of management which foots the bills.

McDonald's views of strikes differ sharply from those of the old-timers. While supporting this fundamental right, he is a stronger champion of negotiation:

"The right to strike is a necessary device. I don't believe man should have to work under employers' conditions unless democratic vote decides that he should do so.

"A strike is a device a working man sometimes has to use to convince the employer that negotiation is a better device. I'm a great believer in the use of negotiation. I believe strikes usually are caused by lack of desire of the employer to continue negotiating.

"Also, I believe most so-called strikes are really lockouts because of the need to firm up market prices.

"With the exception of the great coal strikes, most strikes are merely suspensions of work. This was true of the so-called great steel strike of 1952. It was mostly a suspension of work to firm up steel markets.

"We should negotiate without the fight. A strike is like a war. You beat each other's brains out and then still have to sit down and negotiate.

"If somebody wants to firm up the price and get us to strike, to hell with them. We won't take the black eye. We'll give them the slowdown. Let them take the black eye or the bloody nose. If they want a lockout, let them have a lockout. They're smart enough."

Although inclined to be philosophical, this closing thrust is an example of how practical the Man of Steel can be.

As he sums it up: "I meet today's problems today, but always with an eye to the future."

Dave rarely assaults management with the hackneyed charges that the old-style labor leaders still employ, even though the basis for those charges expired with the Roosevelt era.

Instead of kicking his way through the door, he more often charms his way in. Soft-spoken like John L. Lewis and Philip Murray until riled, he can turn on the steam and cuss like the steelworker that he is.

161

Measuring up to Lewis and Murray in ability to pull out the dramatic stops, Dave differs in that he resembles the polished and erratic John Barrymore rather than the fire-spouting William Jennings Bryan or spellbinding Billy Graham.

Patrick Fagan, Pittsburgh City Councilman and former United Mine Workers official who was closely associated with McDonald in his climb up the labor ladder, sketches this view of him:

"McDonald is a very good executive. He has the qualifications, intellect and ability to do an outstanding job.

"He is experienced and had the great benefit of training under a man like Phil Murray. In steel, he was Murray's right arm during the tough organizing period.

"Throughout the long negotiations in the steel industry, Murray had him at his side, furnishing facts, operating the slide-rule and helping write the contracts. Dave made the classifications of jobs both for coal and steel.

"In the first contract negotiations of steel entirely on his own last Spring (1953), McDonald really did an outstanding job.

"Dave knows that bargaining has to be 50-50. He knows that it can't be 70-30 or 30-70 and is willing to carry out both the letter and spirit of the contract.

"His word is his bond. His belief and philosophy is that a contract is a sacred obligation and that both sides should live up to it.

"While fighting for the people he has the honor to represent, he gives the benefit of doubt to the other side. If his people are wrong, he's just as firm with them as he is with an employer.

"Dave makes an excellent speech, has a fine command of the language and grammar and can hold an audience with the best of them."

The New Look in labor measures up to his role in appearance, as well as in ideas and actions.

Nearing his 51st Birthday (November 22, 1953), McDonald resembled anything but the popular conception of a labor leader. He looked more like a college football coach, big, broad-shouldered, blue-eyed, handsome with wavy silver-white hair.

Unlike the old-style labor leaders, who thought the members wanted them to put up a "poor front," this man of steel dresses to fit the occasion and in keeping with the growing prestige of labor. While seeking the best possible in life for the steelworkers, he believes their officers should set the pace by putting their best foot forward. He goes first-class everywhere.

Although favoring sports outfits and tweeds with bow-ties, he wears "Brooks Brothers" business suits when conservative clothes are in order.

His strenuous, unending round of union business, civic, social and sports activities has kept his figure to a solid 200 pounds—plus.

However, the heavy strain of the Steelworkers' presidency, unceasing demands on the banquet circuit and

163

more worries than a big-league baseball manager are exacting their toll. Deep lines are etched on his Irish face and an occasional nervous twitch of the head shows the constant pressure under which he lives.

The chronic complainers and free-ride experts close in on him much like they do in other fields.

Still a striking figure, he is equally at home and welcomed in millionaire clubs like Pittsburgh's austere Duquesne Club, as well as in union halls. Some snipers object to his crossing the lines, but it has helped promote understanding in the big picture of labor-management relations.

Off the public stage, Dave alternately is smooth and suave or rough and tumble. A "ham actor" at heart, who pulls out all the stops learned during his drama studies at Carnegie Tech, he turns the charm off and on depending on the mood or purpose.

This makes for a sort of "Jekyl-Hyde" personality that perplexes people. Frequently it is hard to tell whether he is acting or playing it straight. He is easy to know and admire, but at times hard to understand and like.

With all of his vanity and maneuverings, the man McDonald can be highly personable, sharp-shooting, deft and efficient in handling an amazing load of activities in a variety of fields.

He can tell a story with the best of them, stay up all night with cronies and spin them off until dawn.

164

A fine change-of-pace conversationalist, he shifts from one subject to the next in machine-gun fashion.

What does he like?

"I love my pipes and I like good cigars . . . and bourbon whiskey is the greatest boon to mankind."

Politics?

"I don't give a damn about labels, Democratic or Republican. Who is this man and what will he do to eliminate poverty? That is the basic question to ask any political candidate."

An objective in life?

"I want to find the little guy who made Julius Caesar tick and the little guy who made Napoleon tick . . . There are unsung heroes and oversung bums."

Although professing that the candidate is more important than the party label, Dave consistently has sided with Democrats. The fact that he is regularly outvoted by a 10-to-1 margin in his home community of Mt. Lebanon in Pittsburgh's suburban South Hills, where Republicans have ruled through bad and good times, hasn't discouraged him a bit.

The Man of Steel also backed two losers in his own party as district delegate to the 1952 Democratic convention in Chicago. Firm friend of President Truman, whom he supported in the 1948 convention, McDonald held out for him even after the President declined to run. His second choice was W. Averell Harriman. The union leader opposed Adlai Stevenson's nomination "because his civil rights program was weak and because of his stand on the Taft-Hartley Act."

Once the campaign got rolling, however, Dave actively supported Stevenson, joining the CIO's political action group in throwing his full weight behind him.

After General Dwight D. Eisenhower's record-smashing triumph, Dave still was without a winner but insisted that "labor did get out the vote." Pointing out that Stevenson received as many votes as Roosevelt in 1940 and Truman in 1948 in winning campaigns, he explained:

"There were more voters and it was these new voters and the women who swung the victory to Eisenhower. It was a great personal triumph for Ike, not a party victory."

Even with his Democratic record, McDonald was appointed by President Eisenhower in 1953 to serve on the U.S. Commission on Economic Foreign Policy.

This Commission was empowered to make recommendations to Congress on foreign aid and related matters. The appointment, backed by Pennsylvania Republican Senators and GOP Congressman James Fulton, from his own district, came in recognition of the high stature of McDonald in international affairs.

The Man of Steel has a remarkable record of hitting to all fields.

His appearance at the 38th annual convention of the Pennsylvania Chamber of Commerce in Pittsburgh's Hotel William Penn, October 22, 1952, marked the first time that the Chamber invited a labor leader to share the platform with businessmen. His afternoon address followed a luncheon talk by Benjamin F. Fairless, Board Chairman and Chief Executive Officer of United States Steel.

These rivals of the bargaining table teamed up again on January 23, 1953 at the "Man of the Year" banquet sponsored by the Pittsburgh Junior Chamber of Commerce. Fairless received the 1952 "Man of the Year" award for his outstanding 15-year record as head of United States Steel, an American success-story rise from newsboy to top man in industry.

McDonald received the first *Philip Murray Memorial Award* for outstanding leadership in the field of labor.

Recalling that Murray had won the first "Man of the Year" award in 1940, Dave paid this unusual compliment to Industrialist Fairless:

"It is indeed fitting that tonight a worthy foe, a hard fighter but a clean one, should receive that same honor.

"I am sure Mr. Fairless misses Mr. Murray like all of us do. They fought often over the bargaining table, but there was a mutuality of respect which marks the character of men sincerely interested in the welfare of the nation."

Extending a similar hand of friendship, the head of U.S. Steel said in accepting the award:

"During a wage dispute, labor leaders may say things about us which make us boil under the collar, and we, in turn, may be a bit intemperate in our remarks about them. But once a settlement is reached we can—and do—close ranks and work together."

167

It was an encouraging step in the direction of peace on the labor-management front.

Again, on the death of Senator Robert A. Taft, author of the Taft-Hartley Act, the head of one of the nation's strongest bodies of organized labor showed his balance in this tribute:

"We in the Steel Workers were extremely sorry to hear of the death of Senator Taft. While our views did not always coincide with his, we always held him in a great measure of respect.

"The United Steel Workers recognized in Senator Taft a man of outstanding ability who expended every ounce of his energy to help promote the welfare of his nation.

"He was a leader and he was a statesman in the true sense of the word. He always fought on a lofty plane for what he believed was right.

"Senator Taft will long be remembered on the pages of his country's history."

Taking part in a wide range of civic activities, McDonald made his weight felt in almost every type of company.

In Pittsburgh's 1941 United Fund drive, he was Chairman of the education committee, heading up the labor group. He was board director and secretary (1949) of the Allegheny County Community Chest; director of the county organization of Boy Scouts, Roselia Foundling Home, American Heart Association, American Cancer Society, National Conference of Christians and Jews, and of the American Arbitration Association.

Dave was one of the original sponsors of the Allegheny Conference on Community Development—the civic group that sparked the billion dollar rebirth of Pittsburgh since the war.

In Pittsburgh's smoke control drive, which cleared the way for the vast rebuilding program, Dave secured the support of CIO officials for the Pittsburgh Smoke Committee, headed by City Councilman A. L. Wolk. The union leader also was secretary of the Steel City Industrial Unions Council which endorsed the sky-cleaning program. And he campaigned for smoke elimination at the annual meeting of the Civic Club of Allegheny County.

The support of labor played an important role in freeing Pittsburgh of its choking smog. Psychologically, the smoke in the city's skies always had been associated with prosperity. And it was a tough job breaking down the impression that smoke was a necessary evil.

McDonald is sincerely active in religious affairs. In January of 1948, he spoke at the 15th annual conference of the National Religion and Labor Foundation in Pittsburgh on the subject, "What Religion Means to Me."

To him, organized religion and organized labor have many common goals. Their relationship, summed up for a religious publication in August of 1953:

"Organized religion and organized labor always run parallel, often merging in the same path.

"Our American labor movement is profoundly religious in its roots. Its passion for justice and its concern for the welfare of the individual come from these religious roots. America's labor leaders are glad because of the interest that religion has taken in labor.

"It is to the advantage of all of us that the worker raise his eyes to God and refuse to concentrate solely on his material welfare. In a godless society, there would be no labor unions because then who would love his fellow man? Who would thirst for justice?"

Dave is particularly interested in the work that the Jesuits (a teaching and missionary order of Catholic priests) are doing in underprivileged countries throughout the world:

"I really admire the Jesuits' efforts in labor education and work in underprivileged countries throughout the world. I have given them everything I could in the way of information, advice and service."

Constantly in demand for speeches, he talks one day about discrimination at a Jewish Labor Committee Conference and the next about the needs and services of the public schools at a meeting of the American Federation of Teachers.

Almost always on the go, his civic interest was recognized by appointment to membership on the public authority formed in 1953 to build a municipal auditorium in Pittsburgh.

When he's not on a special assignment in Washington for the State Department or somewhere else in the U.S., chances are he'll be steaming abroad on a labor mission.

The ocean-hopping has taken him everywhere but the Orient.

Once an avid reader of everything from brain-twisting engineering textbooks to Shakespeare, Dave, since taking over the union Presidency, has had little time for more than a quick flip through newspapers and magazines.

Perhaps his greatest outside love is sports. He never seems to be able to get his fill of football, baseball and boxing.

"The Pirates, of course, are my favorite baseball team," he confesses, "with the Cardinals a close second. I'm a great admirer of Cardinal Manager Eddie Stanky. He was a wonderful player and just as good a manager."

The Cardinal view is understandable, but saying what he did about the Pirates, after their dismal 1952–53 campaigns, took real love.

From his Forbes Field box, behind the dugout, McDonald enjoyed kidding the players, and getting it right back.

In football, his interest runs to the pros "who put on the best show." He knew all the old Chicago Bears of the Bronco Nagurski, Joe Stydahar, Bulldog Turner, and Sid Luckman eras.

Feats of his own boy, though, make even the pros pale in contrast. Davey, Jr., 13, played tackle for St. Bernard's unbeaten team that won the 1952 Pittsburgh Catholic Grade School League championship.

In 1953, Davey moved up to Mellon Junior High

School in Mt. Lebanon. Although a sturdy 150-pound lineman, he was outweighed considerably in this league.

"Ah yes, he's in the big league now," the elder McDonald explained with a burst of paternal pride. "He's in there playing with boys 20 and 30 pounds heavier. But he still does a pretty good job and is a better athlete than his Dad ever was."

When Mellon Junior High dropped a 12-6 decision to Bethel Junior High, the bad news was cabled to the elder McDonald aboard ship en route to Europe. More people heard about that dire result and how unhappy it made the McDonald family than they did about the Notre Dame score or any other game played that same day.

On the golf course, the man of steel is something less than wonderful—and says so.

"Very lousy," he concedes, "I just don't work at the game enough."

With a cultivated slice, he usually manages to break 100 and posted a best score of "mebbe 92."

But he still knows his way around the squash and handball courts.

Along with sports, Dave qualifies as an amateur photographer, having developed and printed "14 zillion pictures and slides."

Another big interest is music—everything from longhair to jive. A regular symphony concert and Broadway musical patron, he was responsible for sending the Pittsburgh Symphony Orchestra on a tour of steel towns in the Pittsburgh area during the 1953 season.

The concerts were sponsored by the steelworkers union with the aim of bringing the best in music to the men in the mills.

In his leisure time at home, Dave likes to fool around at the piano playing "some Basin Street and a little jive." He took up jazz piano in 1940. His theme song is *St. Louis Blues.*

The Steelworkers' official also is an author, teaming up with Eddie Lynch in writing *Coal and Unionism,* the history of the United Mine Workers of America, in 1940.

With his pretty wife, Rosemary, and son, Davey, Mc-Donald lives in an eight-room stone home at 820 Ridgeview Drive in the Hoodridge section of Mt. Lebanon, in suburban Pittsburgh.

He drives a shiny dark blue Cadillac sedan, late model, but still enjoys a good hike with "Pepsi," powerful brown boxer given to his son, Davey, for a 1952 Christmas gift.

Taking "Pepsi" out is about equal to a union-hall tussle. After a romp one day in the early fall of 1953, the Man of Steel, with his green gabardine trousers and contrasting gray coat rumpled, and straining to hold onto the leash, concluded unhappily:

"I'm afraid we'll have to get rid of Pepsi. I'm not home enough to take care of him. Young Davey is too busy with football and other things. And this is just too much dog for Rosemary to handle."

CHAPTER 13

FOR THE FUTURE

IN HIS plush brown and green office on the 15th floor of Pittsburgh's Commonwealth Building, Dave McDonald carries out the daily demands of his job.

Each day a pile of correspondence accumulates on his desk and he methodically sifts through it—scribbling an answer on the margin of a letter or barking into the dictaphone for the longer replies.

Seldom is he without a line of callers.

Someone may want a donation for a charity drive.

A steelworker may have a personal problem that cannot be solved on the local level.

Most of the callers are on official union business. And Dave takes them all in stride.

As he talks with a visitor, he has the knack of juggling messages and phone calls—then returning to pick up the thread of conversation just where it was broken off.

174

His secretary, Kitty Duhig, feeds him the cues and he rarely muffs one. In the Washington office, with Molly Lynch as secretary, the pace may be slower—but more intense. The problems there are often on the national or international level.

It is only on long trips that he gains a breathing spell from his busy desk, the convention floor or the always hectic bargaining sessions.

He especially benefits from the frequent sea voyages which he must take in connection with his work in the international field.

Even then he is restless. He paces the deck. He talks to stewards, waiters, businessmen, dowagers, young girls, old men—all with equal ease and charm. He dances in the lounge. He throws down a drink of bourbon or scotch in a hurry.

Nothing is done leisurely.

One day in October, 1953, aboard the S.S. *United States,* bound for Scotland to establish memorials to the late Philip Murray and Allan Haywood, CIO immortals, he paused in his first-class suite long enough to sum up his views of the future and reflect on the past.

Without any "ifs" or "buts" McDonald predicted that the two major federations and the "walk-out" miners' union would team up for labor unity:

"The CIO and AFL are going to become one labor association—and the UMW will be part of it. As for Reuther [CIO President], he will still be President of the United

175

Auto Workers. We want unity and intend to get it so that we can organize more people."

This came on the heels of his 1953 Labor Day pledge for labor unity of all workers, an August denial of a rumored coal-steel merger and persistent reports he would pull the USA out of the CIO to form a third labor movement.

Of the drive for a guaranteed annual wage, he declared himself, saying that it is both necessary and possible:

"So, we'll get it. Not only is it economically possible, but economically necessary. We'll do it, but I'll set no target date. We must shape the future for it.

"The guaranteed annual wage is needed to wipe out fear of depression and poverty. If people begin to feel insecure, they will freeze up. And if they freeze up, they will stop buying things. If they stop buying things, we will have a depression. The guaranteed annual wage will give them a feeling of security.

"President Eisenhower should revive the study of the guaranteed annual wage started by Franklin Roosevelt. He owes that to the American people. He should at least put his blessing on it.

"If the people even think they are secure, they will spend their money. And if they spend their money, the wheels of industry will continue to turn.

"Of course, the guaranteed annual wage puts a tremendous obligation on salesmanship in the industries. But it puts the job in private hands instead of in a socialized state."

176

The GAW, as it is known, long has been sought by the Steelworkers. It was proposed as early as their first convention in 1937 when no fewer than 15 resolutions were introduced. In 1943, it formally became part of the union program in collective bargaining.

Only the wage provisions were up for consideration in 1953. With the full contract expiring July 1, 1954, the GAW loomed as the major issue.

Along with this, McDonald said employers should provide the difference between workmen's compensation benefits and what the worker would get if he were on the job, free family social insurance (health-hospitalization), higher pensions divorced from Social Security benefits.

Refusing to predict just what shape the GAW will take or what goals lie beyond that, he said:

"It is a question of what the industries can stand. The ultimate? Who knows? Who can call the things to come? My grandfather came to America to work for $1 a day. My father came to cut the load of the work week from 84 to 40 hours. I am now working for the guaranteed annual wage.

"Beyond that, organized labor should strive to achieve those things, whatever they may be, which will be best for the individual, this country and the world."

In McDonald's mind, the future holds many things for the working man for which he will not have to bargain:

177

"We are on the threshold of the greatest industrial revolution mankind has ever known. I believe that through uses of the newfound sciences of electronics and atomic energy, we can eliminate most of the strain and burden that now lie on man's shoulders and arms.

"As the steam engine did so much for man, electronics and atomic energy can relieve almost all of the burdens from men's backs and put the burdens on men's minds."

McDonald cites the steel industry as an example of what has happened in the mid-twentieth century:

"A roller once stood out in front of the mill, grabbed a piece of steel with tongs and shoved it through a set of rolls. Today the roller watches electronic gauges and pushes buttons.

"While the physical effort has diminished, his mental effort has increased. Consequently, his contribution to the welfare of mankind has increased."

Turning to the Scriptures to support this idea of change, he explained:

"When God said, 'You shall earn your bread by the sweat of your brow,' he didn't necessarily mean heaving and hauling with muscles—but heaving and hauling with your brain, as well.

"There always will be plenty of jobs," he concluded. "except that they will change from physical to mental. There always will be 'drawers of water and hewers of wood.' Someone always will have to line the furnaces and line the ladles. They can't line themselves. However, with

178

all of these new things coming, there will be more white collar jobs."

Taking a final look at the advancing machine age, Mc-Donald came up with this brain-twister:

"No matter what the machine may be, man must build it, keep it operating and man must repair it. Machines can build machines but man must build into machines the ability to build machines.

"A machine can think, but only to the extent that man can build the ability to think into the machine. A machine can never learn anything new. It can never create a thought. It can only think what a man has told it to think."

On the subject of world peace, McDonald had equally positive views:

"War is just like a strike. Why hit one another over the head with an A-Bomb and kill millions of people when, at the end, you still have to sit down and negotiate? Why not sit down and negotiate before you fight and keep negotiating if it takes 100 years. Sit down and do it."

However, McDonald does not believe this could be done the way it was being attempted in the Fall of 1953:

"It can't be done through the United Nations, but by the United States and Russia sitting down and negotiating. By constant and continual prayer, by constant and total diplomacy . . . it can be done . . . it takes both prayer and diplomacy."

179

As a world traveller, constantly sowing the seeds of unionism, he believes labor can play a major role in international affairs:

"American labor can sell other countries on the gains that have been made here. I have been trying to tell world labor to do for itself what government cannot do for it.

"This is the way we can sell the United States to other people better than any way we have tried and fumbled in the past."

As the shipboard interview drew to a close, McDonald took a backward look over his career in the labor movement.

"My fight," he said, "has been against poverty in the United States, in Europe, in South America—every place I have found it. When I think of those poor fellows in Chile, Colombia and places like that . . . living out on the pampas and on great deserts and mountains . . . where life expectancy is around 24 to 25 years . . . where their sole ambition is the hope of some day having enough money to buy a bicycle . . . I see the reason why the world is constantly troubled.

"You don't know what it is to be poor unless you have been poor and I was poor . . . then you know why every working man should belong to a union . . . this is a thing so deep and profound in me that it is hard to say in words . . .

"If the people of America only believed enough in the fundamental principles of the American Revolution and worked hard enough to support them, Communism would be a sitting duck.

" 'We hold these truths to be self-evident . . . that all men are created equal.' That and Christ's 'Love thy neighbor as thyself,' are the two greatest statements ever made in the history of mankind."

Summing up his own career, the Man of Steel gazed out a porthole and said:

"The greatest influence on McDonald has been McDonald. You have to believe things and feel things for yourself. My mother and father were greater influences on me than Lewis, Murray, Green, Gompers and all the others in the labor movement put together.

"Why do I have to believe in anybody except Christ?

"I have a mind of my own. I think for myself. My mother and my father, they believed in this thing. They believed in unionism.

"Lewis and Murray influenced my mind, of course. But they didn't change it one bit."

There isn't much more a man of destiny can say. But Dave McDonald had a final word.

"Steel is a funny thing," he mused. "I remember my first day at National Tube. I went down into the mill. Right in front of me a 50-foot piece of half-inch tubing leaped out of a trough. It was white hot and missed me by a foot. It could have drilled right through me had I have taken one more step.

"But, it missed."